THE SWORD AND THE ANVIL

A definitive guide for natural, healthy healing from Post-Traumatic Stress and Trauma.

Robert Serocki, Jr.

ONE WORLD PRESS
Chino Valley, Arizona

Copyright © 2016, Robert Serocki, Jr.

All rights reserved. No part of this book may be reproduced in any manner without written permission from the publisher, except in the case of quotes used in critical articles and reviews.

ISBN: 978-1-938043-18-5

This book was published in the USA by:

ONE WORLD PRESS
890 Staley Lane
Chino Valley, AZ 86323
800-250-8171
PrintMyBook@OneWorldPress.com
www.oneworldpress.com

From manuscript to book in 60 days.
production@oneworldpress.com

"Because of your sword, you have become a slave to the anvil."

The Author

*"Take time to heal, become inspired, move forward
and
BE successful with your life!"*

The Author

Robert Serocki, Jr's current publications include, *A line in the Sand: The true story of a Marine's experiences on the front lines of the first Gulf War* and *Chrysalis: A Metamorphosis Has begun!* These two books are about his life and his experiences as a Marine in combat and afterwards, when he was dealing with and overcoming Post Traumatic Stress (PTS). It's a process that took him six years to complete after suffering from its debilitating effects for more than 20 years. Through this process, he became the 23rd Veteran. To The one who chose life. On several occasions, Robert has spoken about the healing qualities his inspiration of writing can offer. He also hosted his own radio show called 23rd Veteran, which was about Veteran issues with a focus on healing, education and uniting the Veteran community. He also gives presentations and consultations about his 13 step foundation to healing in order to help people completely transform their lives.

You can find out more about Robert Serocki, Jr. by going to his website www.robertserocki.com

The author of this book does not dispense medical advice or prescribe the use of any technique as a form of treatment for physical, emotional, or medical problems without the advice of a physician, either directly or indirectly. The intent of the author is only to offer information of a general nature and to provide some insight in order to help you in your journey toward emotional healing. If any individual uses any of this information in this book for yourself, which is your constitutional right, the author and the publisher assume no responsibility for your actions.

DEDICATION

This book is dedicated to all those whom suffer from Post-Traumatic Stress and trauma. Know that this is a temporary condition from which you can most definitely heal. How long you suffer from it is entirely dependent upon you. By reading this book you have displayed courage to face your trauma and that has inspired me. I desire that my book will in turn inspire you.

Robert Serocki, Jr.
23rd Veteran/Author
www.robertserocki.com

"Everyone has the ability to dream… But not everyone commits to making their dreams reality! The world is your oyster!"

The Author

INTRODUCTION

By now you are probably wondering what 23rd Veteran is? There are 22 Veterans that commit suicide every day in this country. That's 8,030 Veterans dying every year! More Veterans are dying from suicide in this country than they are from the current wars in Afghanistan and Iraq.

The medical community in general is not prepared to handle these Veterans. The Government has turned their backs on their Veterans. The military is discharging them for having Post-Traumatic Stress (PTS). A condition they developed fighting for our country. So where do these young men and women turn now before they become another statistic?

I am the 23rd Veteran. The one who chose life. After serving four years in the Marine Corps and two tours of duty on the front lines in the first Gulf War, I suffered from PTS for more than 20 years. I lost everything. I lost a very good job of nearly 20 years, two homes, my friends, my family, ended up in a wheelchair and ended up in two different hospitals because I wanted to end my life twice.

After being through both the civilian and VA medical systems, I decided enough was enough. I was going to heal. Things had to change. I accepted responsibility for my life. Once I did that I was able to change it for the better by making different choices in order to get the results I desired. I embarked on a journey of self-reliance, awareness, positive thinking and natural, healthy healing practices. Now, eight years later I am alive and well AND I am here to tell you about it.

Change, healing and thus life can be difficult. No one's life is immune to this. It's about how we all deal with and perceive our adversity. Do we overcome it and learn from it in order to become successful, whatever success is to the particular individual? Or, do we succumb to it? As you participate in your journey make sure to take time to reward and honor yourself. Be proud of yourself for ALL of your gains no matter how small you think they are. They will build in size and structure with time. Always be sure to give yourself breaks along the way and rest. You will need it.

Your healing will be a time consuming process and it is dynamic. Success and the accomplishment of your goals is a lifetime process. Healing, growing and learning should never stop. With all of my books, *A line in the Sand*, *Chrysalis* and this book, I hope to help you achieve your goals. These books can be a reference for you as you move forward along your path. This is something I felt strongly about providing to people because as I went through my journey I had books that told me how to do things, but I never found a book that showed me what it was like to actually go through the process. I always thought that if I would have had that, I would have moved along my path faster because I would not have given up so many times thinking that I was doing the wrong thing and having bad reactions. I would have known those reactions were a normal part of the process and I was actually on the right path! So, with my books I am committed to providing that unique reference for you.

A lot of this book is based on personal research, my life experiences and the application of what I learned from those endeavors towards the attainment of my goals. One of the things I wanted to accomplish was to place the plethora of information that is available on PTS and healing into one convenient location that is easily accessible for all, such as this book.

If you do not have a copy of my books, you can simply go to my website www.robertserocki.com. They will help you along your way. Thank you for taking the first step in your journey towards healing. As more people come on board and accomplish this, the world can only be a better place! Together we can help anyone heal. Happy reading and good luck in your journey!

Robert Serocki, Jr.
23rd Veteran/Author
www.robertserocki.com

POST TRAUMATIC STRESS (PTS) TIMELINE

1900 B.C.: Egyptian physicians first report hysterical reactions.

8th Century B.C.: Homer's Odyssey describes the "travails of Odysseus," a veteran of Trojan Wars, including flashbacks and survivor's guilt.

490 B.C.: Herodotus writes of a soldier going blind after witnessing the death of a comrade next to him.

1597: Shakespeare vividly describes war sequelae (Lady Percy in King Henry IV).

1600: Samuel Pepys describes symptoms in survivors of the Great Fire of London.

1678: Swiss military physicians diagnose "nostalgia," the first term to describe what would eventually be recognized as PTSD.

1700s: French surgeon Dominique Jean Larrey identifies three stages of what would eventually become known as PTSD.

1855: Dorthea Dix's advocacy efforts lead to the opening of the Government Hospital for the Insane, and military physicians begin documenting mental issues among Civil War soldiers.

1879: Johannes Rigler coins term compensation neurosis.

1880's: Pierre Janet studies and treats traumatic stress and eventually describes "hysterical and dissociative symptoms, inability to integrate memories, biphasic nature" of suppression and intrusion, and other symptoms often resulting from abuse.

1890's: Sigmund Freud believes patients' memories of abuse and develops seduction theory, which relates symptoms to traumatic sexual experience. Unfortunately, within a few years, he recants in favor of the theory that patients' accounts are just fantasized sexual desires.

1899: Helmut Oppenheim coins term traumatic neurosis.

1905: The Russian Army recognizes "battle stress" as a medical condition.

1914: The term "shell shock" is coined to describe an assumed link between nervous and mental shock among British soldiers in World War I.

1917: Congress initiates plan to shift veteran's compensation from a gratuity to an indemnity for physical and mental disabilities.

1919: Amendments clarify the new benefits for those whose service has impacted the veteran's ability to work, instituting a policy of determining cash payments and services provided based on the percentage of impairment.

1922: The British government's "report of the War Office Committee of Inquiry into Shell-Shock" includes early treatment recommendations.

1939: U.S. military terminology begins to refer to the condition as "combat exhaustion."

World War II: The terms battle fatigue, combat exhaustion, and traumatic neurosis are used to describe symptoms thought to be caused primarily by the stress of combat.

1943: A psychiatrist is added to the table of organization of each division of the military to address increased mental issues in the armed forces during World War II. Gen. George S. Patton is relieved of duty after slapping two soldiers recuperating from "combat stress" in a military hospital.

1945: U. S. Army training film for medical officers recommends sodium pentothal and suggestive therapy as treatments for combat exhaustion.

1946: The National Mental Health Act expands mental health facilities in the U.S.

1952: The first edition of the American Psychiatric Association's Diagnostic and Statistical manual of Mental Disorders (DSM-1) includes "gross stress reaction."

1965: Military battalions begin to include officers to treat psychological issues during the war in Vietnam.

1968: The DSM-II drops "gross stress reaction."

1972: A New York Times op-ed by psychiatrist Chaim Shatan raises public awareness of "post-Vietnam syndrome."

1979: The first Vet Centers are established to aid Vietnam War veterans facing "readjustment problems" that would later be identified as PTSD. Outreach expands to include veterans of World War II and the Korean War.

1980's: The False Memory Foundation urges caution in some cases of trauma since memories can change over time.

1980: PTSD is added to the third edition of the Diagnostic and Statistical Manual of Mental Disorders (DSM-III).

1987: Diagnostic criteria revised in DSM-III-R, dropping the requirement that stressors be "outside the range of normal human experience."

1991: Sertraline-brand name Zoloft-is approved by the US Food & Drug Administration (FDA) as safe and effective for treatment of major depression. This class of selective serotonin reuptake inhibitors (SSRIs) is one of the first medications to receive FDA approval for the treatment of PTSD. Dr. George Everly coins the term psychotraumatology to describe the study of traumatic experience and the prevention and treatment of symptoms.

1994: Diagnostic criteria revised in DSM-IV.

2000: Diagnostic criteria revised in DSM_IV_TR.

2009: Foa, Keane, Friendman and Cohen publish "Effective treatments for PTSD, Second Edition, "a comprehensive book on treatment of PTSD detailing therapeutic approaches and successes with cognitive-behavioral therapy and medication.

2013: Diagnostic criteria revised in DSM-V. It is no longer categorized as an anxiety disorder and is now in a new category, trauma-and stressor-related disorders.

2016: Serocki, Jr., Robert A. Marine and Gulf War Veteran, publishes, "The Sword and the Anvil: A guide for natural, healthy healing from Post-Traumatic Stress and trauma."

Sources: U.S. Department of Veterans Affairs (ptsd.va.gov) History of PTSD website (historyofptsd.wordpress.com), Wikipedia, http://on.pnj.com/1w3ZoK9, The Post Traumatic Stress Disorder Sourcebook Second Edition: A guide to healing, recovery and growth (Glenn R. Schiraldi, Ph.D. [2009])

"Sometimes in my bed at night I curse the dark and pray for the light and sometimes the lights no consolation. Don't you know me I am the boy next door, the one you found so easy to ignore? Is that what I was fighting for? No!"

Huey Lewis and the News

POST TRAUMATIC STRESS (PTS)

CHAPTER 1

What is Post Traumatic Stress (PTS)? Well, it's a little different for each individual. Your experience with PTS will vary depending on the type of trauma you experienced, your personality, your individual genetic makeup and upbringing. However, there are certain symptoms that every person who develops PTS will experience.

PTS is labeled as a disorder. Is it really? Basically a disorder disturbs the order of, or regular normal function of something. So in that definition, yes, PTS would be a disorder. However, it can also be described as an abnormal physical or mental condition. In that definition PTS is not a disorder because it is a perfectly normal reaction to abnormal events in your life. Albeit, genetics can lend to developing PTS but they certainly are not the main root of it. Obviously, there are some inconsistencies here just as you will find there are with treating the condition. Furthermore, the "condition" can turn into a disorder in the sense that if you do not properly treat it, you will suffer from it the rest of your life.

A lot of people say that they lose jobs or can't get one because they have been labelled with having an abnormal disorder. However, companies ethically and legally cannot fire or not hire you because you have a medical condition. The real issue here, just as it was in my case, is that you most likely cannot get a job, or keep one, because you cannot function in a work environment. Let alone in your daily life. You just have to face that fact. So, the key is to fix the condition first, heal and then go get a job. You will most likely need the time off in order to concentrate on yourself and healing as I had to do. I could not even have a relationship with a person when I was dealing with my healing process. It was too much to cope with at the time and I was having to learn how to function all over again. I do propose we should call it Post Traumatic Stress Condition (PTSC). You can treat a condition. However, let's not focus so much on a letter in a word here. The real issue is dealing with the condition and healing from it, not the semantics of its label. That's just what it is, a label.

For me, suffering from PTS involved being afraid of the dark, panic attacks, jumping from loud noises, having colors and smells thrust me into flashbacks and taking me back to the war. PTS caused me to become a prisoner in my own home. I was afraid to leave the house. I even ordered my groceries on line and had them delivered. I moved my bed up against the wall so it resembled my fighting hole in the Saudi Arabian desert. I sat with my back to the wall in a corner, next to the door in college and spent the entire class trying to figure out how to get out of the classroom in case anything happened. I began having heart palpations, shortness of breath, and a burning sensation in my chest, dizziness and chronic pain. I developed nausea and insomnia, sometimes not sleeping for five days at a time. I didn't know what to do. I thought I was going crazy. I began to self-medicate with copious amounts of alcohol because its effects were almost immediate. I lost my job of 16 years, lost two homes and had to file bankruptcy. I had no way to live, pay bills, or feed myself. Then, after two suicidal ideations and two extended stays in the hospital, I was put on five different kinds of psychotropic medications. This ended up causing a whole new set of health problems because my doctors left me on the medication for six years with no plan of taking me off of them and putting me on a positive path towards a healthy successful life.

    I was forgotten about by my doctors, my family and my friends. I developed skin rashes that wouldn't heal, gained 80lbs, ended up in a wheelchair and I turned into a complete drugged up zombie. Until one day I got fed up with this miserable existence. I was no longer living and I did not like it. I could have just blamed everyone and everything for my problems and kept taking the medication and existing until I died, but I didn't. I took responsibility for my life and the decisions I had made. I realized that I was in the position I was in and going through what I was going through because of the decisions that I had made. Once I came to that realization, I also understood that I could change my life around. You may be asking, "How?" By simply making different decisions. If you don't like the results that you are getting, then you need to make different decisions in order to get different results. I forced myself out of my wheelchair after being in it for two years, I quit all five of my medications at once cold turkey and then I lost 60lbs. From that point on, I have completely changed my life around. I am happy, successful, free and I love life. Now, I pass what I have learned along to you in hopes that you do not have to suffer as long as I did and more importantly, you can get your life back. You can be happy and successful again.

    So, what is PTS? PTS is generally thought of as a traumatic event that occurs in someone's life that has the potential to cause feelings of horror and fear. These feelings, if left untreated, have the potential to consume one's life by taking it over and holding the individual prisoner to it. PTS can cause physical illnesses, such as hypertension, asthma, and chronic pain.

Your trauma can also cause other symptoms, such as heart palpitations, shortness of breath, tremors, nausea, insomnia, unexplained pain and mood swings. The trauma can cause an individual to live in a perpetual state of fear which can overwhelm a person's coping skills and lead them to avoidance behavior. These symptoms can show up shortly after the traumatic event and sometimes they don't show up for quite some time later.

If these symptoms are treated properly when they first occur, they have a tendency to go away. However, if left untreated they will continue growing in magnitude and perplexity for as long as you do not deal with them. This then can cause you to live in a perpetual state of fear and cause you to avoid anything and everything that reminds you of your trauma.

Some of the symptoms of PTS are things like intrusive memories, avoidance, and changes in emotional reactions. The intensity of these symptoms can vary over time and you may experience more symptoms at certain times than others.

Doctors are uncertain why some people get PTS and it is most likely caused by a complex mix of variables and genetics. One of the distinctions they do make is that it's all related to how your brain regulates the chemicals and hormones that your body releases in its response to the stress you are experiencing. This is interesting to me because if you can do things yourself to help regulate these chemicals and hormones in your body then you can help yourself heal from the symptoms of PTS. For instance PTS and stress in general, causes your body to release cortisol which can cause several other health problems. However, you can do healthy, natural things to reduce the cortisol in your body such as drinking black tea and ingesting Omega 3 fish oil. We will discuss this more in another chapter.

As far as treatments are concerned, there are several known types, such as psychotherapy and medications. As far as psychotherapy is concerned there are Cognitive, Exposure and EMDR therapies. There are also two main types of medications. These are antidepressants and anti-anxiety medications. The anti-anxiety medications do have the potential for abuse and are not supposed to be taken on a long term basis.

An individual can also take actions in order to help themselves when dealing with PTS. They can learn about PTS, take care of themselves, don't self-medicate, break the cycle, talk to someone and consider a support group.

In my opinion, the best way you can help yourself is through education. Educate yourselves about PTS and you can help yourself. That is what I did. As with anything in life, one of the biggest keys to success is education. It is the best way to limit risk and cut your losses. In fact, every successful person in history I have read about, and there are a lot of them, stated that the number one key to their success was "education" and to "never stop learning."

The first treatment I had just mentioned is Cognitive Behavioral Therapy (CBT). It has been described as the most effective treatment for PTS. It usually involves meeting with a therapist once a week for 3 to 6 months. I found it very interesting that this is the most effective treatment for PTS, yet it was never offered to me in the six years that I was being treated for it. Furthermore, I could never get an appointment with a doctor any sooner than every two months at best. To top all of that off, the psychiatrist I was seeing, whom was prescribing me psychotropic drugs, stated to me that she did not know anything about counselling, therapy, or psychology!

The second type of therapy I mentioned is Prolonged Exposure (PE) which is a type of CBT where the individual talks about their trauma over and over again until the memories are no longer upsetting. This also was never offered to me or discussed with me. My appointments were only 30 minutes long and I was quite often rushed out of the office after the doctor spent most of my session on small talk instead of the PTS.

Talking about your trauma repeatedly does work. So does writing about it and you can do this yourself in the comfort of your own home. I did both over and over again and it worked wonders for me. In fact, it led to me publishing two previous books on the subject www.robertserocki.com. What you are doing by talking/writing about the trauma is releasing emotionally charged memories in healthy ways not destructive ones. This is done until the memories simply become just memories without the emotion.

The third treatment I mentioned is Eye Movement Desensitization and Reprocessing (EMDR). It usually involves focusing on distractions like hand movements or sounds while you talk about your traumatic event.

The last treatment type involves medications, which are the most widely used method of treatment for PTS by the medical community. The first type is Selective Serotonin Reuptake Inhibitors (SSRI's). They work by raising serotonin levels in your brain so that you feel better. The only two SSRI's that are currently approved by the FDA for PTS are Zoloft and Paxil. Neither of which were ever offered to me. Another type of medication are benzodiazepines. They can be helpful at first, but they do not treat the main PTS symptoms. They can lead to addiction and are not usually recommended for long term PTS treatment. This also is disturbing in that I was given these types of medications right off the bat and I was left on them for six years! The only reason I wasn't on them after that was because I quit them all cold turkey on my own. My doctor was quite shocked when I went into the office and dumped all of the unused medication bottles on the desk and stated that I was done with them and had been off of them for two months. I haven't looked back since.

These therapies were not the "first-line" treatments offered to me. My first-line treatments were five different types of medications. Most of which the medical community warns against using because of the potential side effects and a propensity for addiction.

In fact, the first three forms of therapy were never offered to me when I began my treatment.

There has been some recent concerns about these treatments and patient wait times. Hmmm, really? I can definitely understand that. The PE therapy is actually part of the Cognitive Therapy treatment and in order for it to be effective the patient must be seen once a week for three to six months. In my own experience, I could only be seen once every two months or so for 30 minutes at a time and that 30 minutes never involved any therapy, counselling, or even just talking about my experiences.

Obviously (do I even need to say it?), that is not going to work. The medical community may be aware of these treatments; however, they don't seem to be able to conduct them in a way that would be effective. It is probably an issue involving inadequate staffing levels and perhaps even a lack of available quality medical personnel willing to work for such organizations. I also have to consider the fact that every treatment seems to require medications, frequently multiple types, no matter what and we all know that in the past medications have generated financial contributions to those institutions/individuals whom prescribe them, not to mention the side effects and health issues they cause for the patient.

The second type of therapy (PE) involves the patient talking about their traumatic experience repeatedly, which in turn causes the experience to be less painful and less dominating of the individual's life. There also is homework involved for the patient and that they should visit places that are safe, but that they would normally avoid. Now, I have to say that this does work. I have done these things myself on my own. You can talk to a trusted family member or friend in the comfort of your own home. You actually don't even have to talk about it if you don't want to. You can write about it, which I used quite effectively I might add. You can paint about it, create a song about it, etc. Use the method that works the best for you. Everyone has a talent and/or inspiration. Find yours.

I also visited places I would avoid like the grocery store. I did it in baby steps. I started by driving to the store and parking my vehicle. I did a little more every day until I actually could walk into the store, shop and finally complete the process by waiting in line and checking out without panicking and running out of the store. It worked. Now, I go to all kinds of places and enjoy myself without incident. It takes practice, time and dedication, but it can work for you as it did for me. The fact of the matter is, your success comes from YOU, not from someone or something else. You do not have to be dependent on someone or something else. Your guarantee is you.

The medical communities' aim is to provide several different types of therapies and treatment options; however, they never mention that you can help yourself. Like the bible says, "Give a man a fish and he will have a meal. Teach a man HOW to fish and he will eat for a lifetime." You can conduct these techniques on your own. If someone can learn these techniques and ultimately teach them, then so can you. We all have the same brain. The only real difference is how each of us actually use it. As I like to say, "What do you do with your fear? Do you work to overcome it, or do you let it defeat you?" The answer to this question determines whether you are a success or a failure. Because, realistically speaking, we all experience fear at some point in our lives, but not everyone overcomes it.

I know that when I quit all of my medications and decided to help myself heal naturally, since my doctors were only just medicating me and ruining my health, the first thing out of my doctor's mouth was that they wanted to take me completely off of my benefits. These were benefits that I clearly and justifiably earned fighting for my country. I had no job, no way to pay bills or even eat; however, that did not seem to concern my doctor.

When I originally filed my PTS claim I was told it would be almost two years before it was completed (so I was supposed to go that long without a place to live or any way to procure food). Well, it did in fact take that long. I also had to see a whole other set of doctors whom would make a decision on my claim, if I had PTS or not, even though I was already seeing one of their own doctors who at the time, were already prescribing me several different psychotropic medications for PTS.

There are many other frustrations that face these mental health care providers, such as their lack of control when it comes to monitoring the effectiveness and possible impact of prescriptions. Even after taking several of these medications for six years my PTS was not getting better. In fact, it had become worse. My health declined in the sense that I was 80lbs heavier, in a wheelchair, and had obvious problems with skin rashes that wouldn't heal. My doctor completely ignored the impact these drugs were having on me.

To me, solving this issue is analogous to trying to get rid of a colony of ants (i.e., the PTS). If you never get rid of the queen (i.e., the root/trauma), you never really get rid of the ants (cure the PTS) do you? The ants (the PTS) just keep coming back and you have to keep attempting to treat the problem instead of curing it once and for all.

Exposure therapy, the third type of treatment, actually happens when a person with PTS experiences a flash back from a trigger or reminder during his or her daily routine. You don't have to go to a doctor to induce this as it happens regularly to a person with PTS. In other words, teach them how to deal with it first so they can apply that to when it happens to them on a daily basis when they are not in the doctor's office. When you tell a patient that you're going to "induce the trauma" on their next appointment most of them aren't going to show because that's the very thing they are trying to avoid! Instead, tell them you are going to train them "how" to handle it so that the next time it does happen they can help themselves. More appealing, isn't it?

Medications do not cure the problem. In fact, in some cases after long term use, they make the symptoms worse just like they did to me. This also then creates addiction. I have talked to many people who take anxiety, or other psychotropic medications, and they just cannot quit them. The side effects of such an endeavor are quite overwhelming. I know, I quit five such medications all at the same time cold turkey. The first seven days were one hell of a rollercoaster ride and at times I thought I was going insane. But I was so determined to get off that stuff and heal for good and in a healthy way that nothing was going to stop me. Anything that can cause an addiction like that cannot be good.

Health care providers have stated in the past that they know how to effectively treat PTS and we hear about all these great new techniques they are coming up with, yet a lot of the health care providers are not even competent in evidence-based treatments. Their idea of treatment is dolling out cocktails of medicine to patients that they themselves recommend to avoid because of health risks and the potential for addiction.

Not only is this information disturbing, but it's pretty accurate based on those I have talked to whom go for PTS treatment and my own experiences dealing with the medical system. I will say it again, we need to start learning about PTS ourselves and how to heal from it both naturally and in healthy ways. This idea of just plying people with copious amounts of medications, oh and we will throw in a little so called therapy, just doesn't work. Just recall the suicide rate of Veterans, 22 a day.

Finally, to conclude this chapter, I want to include something that is very important. If you are a person who knows, lives with, friends with, relative of, or works with someone who has PTS you will want to read this list. It is called, The 10 Tips for Understanding Someone with PTSD. I found it on the Heal My PTSD blog site. Here is an abbreviated version of it:

1. Knowledge is Power.
2. Trauma Changes us.
3. PTSD hijacks our identity.
4. We are no longer grounded in our true selves.
5. We cannot help how we behave.
6. We cannot be logical.
7. We cannot just get over it.

8. We're not in denial–we're coping.
9. We do not hate you.
10. Your presence matters.

This is a fabulous list and I found all of this to be true with myself when I was suffering from PTS. So, as bleak as things seem at the moment, this can all be changed by the individual with PTS and of course with your help and support. Veterans and people with PTS already feel like they have been abandoned. So, when their friends and family have also abandoned them, it only exacerbates the problem. This then leads to a total distrust of anyone or anything. My family abandoned me during this time period. If it wasn't for my girlfriend supporting me as I went through my journey, I do not know if I ever would have been able to begin to heal and complete the process. Albeit she is only one person, but sometimes that is all it takes. So, if you only remember one thing on that list of tips, make sure you remember number 10. Just YOUR presence in our lives matters and it means the most to us. Even if we don't say so.

"I can't remember anything, can't tell if this is true or a dream, deep down inside I feel to scream, this terrible silence stops me. Now that the war is through with me, I'm waking up I cannot see that there's not much left of me. Nothing is real but pain now. Hold my breath as I wish for death. Oh god please wake me!"

Metallica

SUICIDE

CHAPTER 2

Now that we have discussed PTS and the medical community, I am going to bring up a very important topic, suicide. It is a possible outcome for those whom have PTS. To exacerbate my point, I will discuss Veteran suicide. This has become a very serious national problem. It has been reported that 22 Veterans commit suicide every day in this country. CNN published this about it, "Every day, 22 veterans take their own lives. That's a suicide every 65 minutes. As shocking as this number is, it may actually be higher." I bring up Veteran suicide to exacerbate my point that you can heal from PTS. However, it has to be in natural, healthy ways. Prescription medications, drugs and alcohol won't cure the problem. They only numb it, create addiction and can possibly lead to suicide. This issue is prevalent in our Veteran community due to a war that has lasted more than a decade and the proliferation of psychotropic drug prescriptions issued, the increased strengths of these medications and the ease at which this condition is diagnosed in the military and after ones service. This issue has been brought out in the open recently, so I am sure you can relate to what I am saying.

This is an important subject to me as I have some experience in this area. However, I am not proud to admit it. You see, as a result of my PTS I contemplated ending my life several times. In fact, I went so far as to load my shotgun twice and put it to my head. Luckily for me, a friend was there on both occasions to interrupt my plans and take me to the hospital. Most Veterans aren't so lucky. That's why this must be discussed. I eventually overcame the PTS and my suicidal ideations and you can too. Or, you may be in a position to help someone else do the same. By the end of this book you will have a foundation to work from in order to help yourself, or someone else heal. But first, let's discuss some issues regarding the growing problem of Veteran suicide.

As I just mentioned, the actual number of Veteran suicides maybe higher. So, now you may be asking yourself just who wasn't counted and why? There are several factors as to why some individuals may not be counted. Such as, the Veterans were not in the VA system or that there is no unified system for reporting these types of deaths in our country. Normally someone like a funeral director or a coroner has to enter a veteran's status and/or suicide on a death certificate. Also, Veteran status is just a single question on the death report and the Defense Department or the VA usually do not verify this.

Furthermore, homeless people may not be counted, or if a veteran intentionally crashes their car or overdoses on drugs or alcohol without leaving a note, they may not be counted. Clearly the statistic of 22 veterans committing suicide every day is most likely much higher.

Another scary point of consideration, which I never really thought about until now, is that a lot of the Veteran suicides were individuals who were age 50 an older. This is most likely because they give up on life once their children are all grown and have moved out, or after a long term marriage falls apart. This then suggests that there may be a huge influx of suicides coming our way.

In August 2012, President Barack Obama signed an executive order calling for stronger suicide prevention efforts. Just a year later, he announced $107 million in new funding for better mental health treatment for Veterans with PTS and traumatic brain injury. Well, after what we just discussed in the last chapter on PTS, we see just how far that got us and how good, proper, quality care is lacking let alone the enormous problem of the under staffing of doctors competent in evidence based treatment therapies that seems to exist. I guess our government just throwing money at the problem doesn't really get us satisfactory results. Veterans are dying because they must wait too long for an appointment. This is all just absolutely appalling.

So, even with the estimate of 22 Veterans dying every day due to suicide, most of the time they never make the news headlines. Transitioning back to life at home after combat is difficult enough as it is. However, the problem is made much worse when these Veterans are forgotten about, abandoned, mistreated and abused by society and especially by the very government they sacrificed their lives for to protect. As I previously stated, that's 8,030 Veterans dying from suicide in any given year. By the end of 2015, after 12 years of war, that's 96,360 Veterans whom will have died due to suicide! This is absurd! What in the world is this country doing wrong? This is completely unacceptable.

Another issue that adds to the complexity of this problem is that once an individual returns home they can lose their sense of serving a greater mission. However, you can still serve a greater mission even if you are not in the military anymore. You have to find your purpose in life, the purpose you made it home from the war for. There is a purpose. For me it was to heal and teach the world what I learned about that process and to use myself as an example. So, based on that purpose, I write my books.

Finding your purpose can be something as simple as an interest you have or your favorite hobby. Find what you are good at and go for it. Do it every day and enhance other people's lives as well as your own. This process is infectious. You will be amazed at how people whom haven't taken that chance yet are inspired by the simple things you do every day. You have to begin to trust yourself again. Once you do that, you will begin to trust others again and build a whole new network for yourself. You will even make all new friends. You just have to focus on the task at hand and don't let yourself be distracted. Of course it isn't easy, but the more you try the more easily you will find it is to catch your focus slipping and you will realize that you are getting off course. You then will be able to refocus and move forward again.

A lot of the Veterans I know with PTS believe their current treatment is ineffective. Somehow I am not surprised here. Of course I am being a bit facetious, but I certainly do understand why a large majority of us Veterans are unhappy and let down by the treatment they do get.

It's no secret anymore that health care at the VA in general, and especially mental health care, is lacking. For most Veterans the VA is their only option. This is true to a certain extent. However, don't forget that you also have yourself. You are your front line defense when it comes to your health care. The more you take care of yourself the better off you will be. Plus, it's relatively inexpensive to do so. Especially with mental health. There are all kinds of healthy, natural things you can do for yourself that will not only improve your mental health, but will improve your over-all health and wellbeing. We will be discussing this in much greater detail in a later chapter of this book. Remember, take care of your brain and it will take care of the rest of you.

The current programs already in place do not really have any positive effect on the numbers of Veterans committing suicide. As we have discussed in this book, the suicide rates are climbing and that number isn't even completely accurate because not all Veteran suicides are actually accounted for. In light of this, the Clay Hunt Bill was passed. It is designed to insure that those who have PTS and are discharged from the military are not done so dishonorably. It also will establish a drug take back program and it will allow the VA to work with Veterans Service Organizations (VSOs) in order to help prevent suicides. The bill is also going to create this pilot program which will repay the student loans for psychiatrists and counselors in an attempt to acquire more doctors and higher quality ones at that. Yet, Veterans can't even get into an appointment any sooner than once a month. Even then, the medical community relies heavily on medication as their primary form of treatment. I could only get an appointment once every two months to see my doctor and I was on five medications at once. So how is this going to actually work?

I think all Veterans should be given the option to seek health care from whomever they wish and it should be covered for them. But see again, no one is talking about the fact that there are things you can do for yourself. Information is everywhere now a days. I decided to write this book in an effort to compile this information. This information is coupled with my own personal experiences and put into one place so that it is easy to acquire and read.

The VA has been criticized for delayed care to Veterans and their own Inspector General and Office of Special Council have found serious and widespread mismanagement and critical breakdowns in treatment. Even with all of this data, it seems as though this very serious problem is being ignored. It is covered up with feel good stories about volunteers or fantastic new state of the art treatment methods when the medical community still cannot properly administer the ones that are currently available.

These issues of inadequate mental health care, mistreatment of Veterans and Veteran suicide have been going on much longer than the current war. The same sort of things happened to me during and after the first Gulf War in 1990/91. The government was forcing us to take drugs that had not been approved by the FDA. During our deployment we were exposed to chemical warfare, given protective suits that didn't work when wet and then told it never happened even though I was gassed five different times by the Iraqi's through artillery shells. I was sent on a suicide mission in order for our government to find out what would happen when we launched our ground attack. We were left out in the desert for a month once the war was over to fend for ourselves until someone remembered we were still out there. Then, once we returned home, we were all ignored and a lot of us hid because we felt so betrayed. We tried to disappear like it all never really happened. Then I decided to go for help. I was put in the hospital for a week at one point. They put me on a bunch of drugs and plopped me in front of a TV in pajamas and just left me there until I demanded to be let out. I felt like I was put in prison simply because I had asked for help because of what my government had done to me and the positions they put me in. The medications caused me to have serious health issues. I was even in a wheelchair for two years. I didn't get better until I decided to heal myself. All of these events are explained in detail in my first two books, *A Line in the Sand*, about my experience in the first Gulf War, and *Chrysalis*, which details my experience dealing with PTS.

Another important issue is the wait times involved before someone who is in dire need of mental health care actually gets to see a doctor. When I contacted the VA about seeing a doctor to get my service connected PTS reviewed, it took them 150 days (5 months!) just to call me back to schedule an appointment almost another month away.

Once I got into the system, I was assigned a constant care provider, but just about every time I called to talk or make an appointment my doctor was on two weeks' vacation. When I did actually get to see the doctor, my doctor would never speak with me about my problems. I was only spoken to about the medications and then the appointment would be over and I was sent on my way.

The VA says they're doing a good job and that they are helping Veterans. They want us to come to them for help, to trust them. Really? After all of this. This is exactly why I wrote this book. I want to help people help themselves. I am doing something the VA/medical community and our government should be doing themselves. In fact, they appear to be causing more harm than good. I am absolutely sick and tired of seeing my fellow Veterans being treated so horribly. That is why I had to try and do something about it.

Even when doctors are interviewed individually (whether government or civilian) they admit that they do not treat mental health, particularly PTS and Veteran suicide, effectively or even properly. They just continue to repeat the same insufficiencies in perpetuity. It is nice, however; to finally start to see some of these doctors speaking out on this massive problem. Now, we just need to take this information and actually do something about it. If you are aware of the problem then you must become part of the solution or you shouldn't complain.

I remember when I was suffering from PTS, I was having serious problems with getting any sleep, let alone enough sleep. Before my first suicidal ideation occurred I was literally lucky if I got an hour of sleep each night. Sometimes, I would go days without sleeping, which made everything a whole lot worse. Then you start self-medicating with things like drugs and alcohol to relax you enough to sleep or even just pass out. Then that leads to a whole other set of problems, which then makes one feel completely useless and miserable which then can lead to thinking of ending one's life just to get a break from this vicious cycle. They are just barely starting to link sleep problems and suicide together as well as considering it a sign that someone may have PTS if they are not already diagnosed with it.

Just about every combat Veteran I know has serious sleeping problems, even if they are heavily medicated and at one time that also included myself. I used to throw kicks and punches in my sleep during my nightmares. One night I woke up after a nightmare because I had actually punched my girlfriend in the back during my nightmare. The sleep drugs did nothing to control my nightmares. They say Prazosin helps that, but I was on that too and it didn't do a thing for me. Even when presented with evidence that this is an issue, some doctors still refuse to link the two or even consider this issue a problem. The only thing that made the nightmares, and eventually the PTS go away, was treating myself with natural, healthy methods without the use of any medications.

Congress passed an act in 2007 in order to address Veteran suicide. It is called the Joshua Omvig Veterans Suicide Prevention Act. Its purpose was to direct the VA to complete a suicide prevention program. So, the VA developed a web-based program to educate its staff about suicide risk as well as how to properly handle someone who had a high risk for suicide. The VA required all of its staff to complete this training by December 30, 2008 or within 90 days of being hired to fill a vacancy of a staff member who was previously trained. Staff were also alerted to inquire about other psychological issues in the person's life like the loss of a job or problems with relationships and that the patient's history of attempting suicide is the biggest predictor of future attempts.

Another act was created in 2008 by congress to deal with the problem of phone calls to suicide hotlines being re-routed, overloading the system and calls from Veterans being put on hold. The VA staff completed the training. In 2012, as I previously mentioned, Barack Obama signed an executive order calling for stronger suicide prevention efforts. A year later he announced $107 million in new funding for better mental health treatment. Furthermore, Congress recently passed yet another bill regarding Veteran suicide (The Clay Hunt Bill).

The VA says they need more money to update their systems, conduct training and hire more qualified staff. Obviously, as I have previously outlined, they have been getting money. So why hasn't this problem gotten any better instead of worse? Again, it's just another let's throw money at the problem to make it look like we are doing something about it and hope it just goes away. Or, just don't do anything at all and pass the buck to some other governmental agency.

"In this reality man is the slave and victim of the machines that have conquered space and time for him; he is intimidated and endangered by the might of the war technique which is supposed to safeguard his physical existence; his spiritual and moral freedom, though guaranteed within limits in one half of his world, is threatened with chaotic disorientation, and in the other half it is abolished altogether."

C.G. Jung
From his book, The Undiscovered Self

PTS ABNORMALITIES

CHAPTER 3

In this chapter we are going to talk about abnormalities and genetics that lend themselves to developing PTS and that may also help protect them when an individual experiences a traumatic event. We will also discuss a little bit about the brain and certain things it needs to function properly in relation to trauma. I will also mention a little bit about acute stress and especially early trauma. If you are going to heal, you must understand how your brain works in relation to experiencing and processing trauma. There is a part of the brain called the amygdala and it discerns between safe and dangerous. This is a protection mechanism enacted by the brain to protect us from any further life threatening circumstances based upon characteristics of "danger" that repeat themselves, which we may notice before the actual dangerous event occurs. In other words, your brain is learning by association in order to prepare you for future fear.

To elaborate on this further, Russian Physiologist Ivan Pavlov conducted experiments on his dogs (i.e., Pavlov's dogs) using a bell and then rewarding the dogs with food once they heard it. The dogs then actually began to salivate when they heard the bell. That then expanded to other sounds similar to the bell. The same could also happen if danger followed the bell.

Your brain records all of this and associates it for further use to your advantage. Just like the experience I had with the color orange. The orange reminded me of the first Gulf war because of the color of the sunsets, sunrises and the explosions of bombs at night. That's where I saw combat. So, every time I saw "orange", no matter what it was, my alert levels automatically rose and I began to panic. Then, my brain began to record everything around me when that happened so all of that then became part of my "danger." For instance, it happened one time I was in my bedroom at sunrise. After that, every time I went in my room I began to panic. So, you can see that if this is left untreated, the problem exacerbates itself and it grows bigger in terms of experiences and magnitude.

The same thing would also happen to me every time I saw a cloudy day. During the ground war it was cloudy and rainy the whole time. So, from there on out every time a cloudy day happened, I panicked. It wasn't until I started paying attention to what was occurring, where it was occurring and the possibilities of why it was occurring, that I started to overcome this. Once I understood why my room was scaring me, I started telling myself that my room was safe and relaxing and there was nothing to fear in there. Then I started re-creating relaxing experiences in my room such as listening to nice music, nature sounds, meditating and reading. After a while, my room and eventually the color orange, stopped bothering me as did cloudy days. You see, once I figured out how and why my brain was recording and thus reacting to these things, I simply started re-training my brain with "good" experiences associated with these stimuli.

See, your brain inherently knows that just one screw up can cost you your life. It's just too risky not to play it safe. Therefore, it reacts with what it deems as an appropriate response. Now then, one can clearly see how this problem becomes so magnified when one experiences a severely traumatic event like combat and then they return home. The problem persists because the individual doesn't properly deal with it and/or no one (i.e., a doctor) helps them properly deal with it. One can also now see how medication isn't a long term solution. It may block this response while you are on it; however, it's not going to cure it. So, when you get off of the medication the problem returns. This is where dependency/addiction steps in. This is also where one starts developing other health problems from being on these types of medications for far too long. You must retrain your brain. Medication and drugs cannot do that for you. It's entirely up to you.

Now that we have talked about the brain a little bit and how it works and processes different positive and negative stimuli, I also want to talk about what I like to call "over activity" of the brain. Think of it as the brain realizing there is real danger and so it over-compensates for that and tries to take control. My hypothesis on over activity is how I explain what happened to me and many other Veterans I have spoken with. I would like to draw your attention to Obsessive Compulsive Disorder (OCD) in order to exacerbate my point.

OCD was something I developed AFTER I began suffering from PTS. When someone has PTS their life and everything in it, feels out of control. Things just happen and you don't know why. Then, it just seems to get worse and worse and as a person you feel like you have totally lost control of your life. You then begin to feel hopeless and your brain over-reacts and tries to take control of your life. I believe it's a survival instinct like fight or flight. This then, in my humble opinion, is where OCD steps in. You begin doing things to effect a good result in your daily life. Funny thing is, do we ever really have control over our fate? It's quite the paradox and an argument I can see going either way depending on one's beliefs and/or ethics. For instance, when I was back in the war they were telling us that 90% of us were going to die the first day. I felt like if I didn't do something to steer the odds in my favor, I would be part of that death toll. So, I began to pray to God every day, several times a day. It helped me feel like I had some control over my life and my fate on the battlefield. I calmed down and even accepted death. Did I really have any control? Some would say yes because I had control over myself to pray to God and hence, because of that, he would protect me. Others would say no and that I simply just tricked myself. I personally fought a war for 20 years that technically only lasted four days. Either way I am still alive, but did I ever really escape the battlefield? Well, yes indeed I have. I can now say that 23 long years later. Was it because I had control? Was it God? Was it because I tricked myself? A little of all three I suppose.

I developed OCD as a result of my PTS. It was a way for me to try and control what was going on. My panic attacks and flashbacks would get so bad sometimes I would literally pass out no matter where I was. So, in order to try and control that I performed rituals. I would check the doors and windows three times each. I would make sure I took seven sips of water. I had to have my chamomile tea every day. I had to say my prayers four times. I had to touch each light switch four times after turning the lights on or off. I kept a rubber band on my wrist to snap it when I started to panic in order to break the cycle. Etc., etc., etc. I kept doing these things until they completely took over my life. I thought if

I kept doing them religiously my "panic" would disappear. Well, that never worked. Things just kept getting worse until I identified and dealt with the root problem, which was my PTS and trauma. It's simple. The PTS was causing every other problem in my life because I was avoiding it, which is also a characteristic of PTS.

I conclude that OCD is a byproduct of having PTS in terms of it being the brain's attempt at controlling negative stimuli, which then becomes a Petri dish that enhances the growth of the need for control over all stimuli because of the possibility of total chaos that exists. This then leads to an individual spiraling out of control at an even more epic rate, when in fact this is what the person was trying to prevent in the first place. Vicious cycle, isn't it?

Your brain precipitates physiological changes within your body in response to stress. One of the things it releases is a stress hormone called cortisol. It is released in the hypothalamus of the brain and this then leads to another chain of events. However, when your body does produce cortisol from chronic stress there are healthy, natural ways to reduce the cortisol levels in the body; helping you to feel better and thus improving your overall health as the cortisol can cause other health problems within your body.

Wikipedia describes cortisol as, "A steroid hormone. It is released in response to stress and a low level of blood glucose. Its primary functions are to increase blood sugar through gluconeogenesis, suppress the immune system, and aid in the metabolism of fat, protein, and carbohydrate. It also decreases bone formation."

It also states that, "Cortisol is released in response to stress, sparing available glucose for the brain, generating new energy from stored reserves, and diverting energy from lower priority activities (such as the immune system) in order to survive immediate threats or prepare for exertion. However, prolonged cortisol secretion (which may be due to chronic stress or the excessive secretion seen in Cushing syndrome) results in significant physiological changes."

Cortisol, as described above, can cause these physiological changes in your body.

- Weakens the immune system
- Reduces bone formation
- Causes collagen loss/inhibits it
- Lengthens wound healing
- Counteracts insulin
- Raises the free amino acids in the serum (decreasing amino acid uptake by muscle)
- Stimulates gastric acid secretion
- Acts as an antidiuretic hormone
- Stimulates many copper enzymes
- Inhibits sodium loss
- Intense potassium excretion
- Works with epinephrine to create memories of short term emotional events (which protects you when the event happens again)

So, it is pretty evident that chronic stress causes the brain to produce cortisol, which then can lead to other physiological changes within our bodies over time. Out of all the doctors I have ever seen, not a single one of them ever mentioned cortisol let alone explain this process. Not one. This is obviously a big key to healing. Obviously you need to try and reduce your stress in order to inhibit this process, but while you are working on that you can also work on lowering your current levels of cortisol in your body. We will go into detail on that in a later chapter where I discuss healthy, natural remedies/techniques for overcoming PTS. Again, I don't understand why a doctor's idea of curing something always must involve some kind of synthetic medication that inhibits or stops a natural occurring process in the body instead of understanding the process and trying to figure out how to deal with it in another natural, healthy way.

A lot of Veterans I have talked to that have PTS also are afflicted with chronic pain. We just discussed how chronic stress produces cortisol in the body and, among other things, it affects bone formation and can cause loss of collagen. This obviously could cause an individual to experience some pain especially in their joints.

So we can see how acute stress, and especially chronic stress, can have negative effects on the human body. Now, couple that with somebody who has PTS and keeps reliving those stressful events, even though they are actually no longer occurring, over very extended periods of time. I suffered with PTS for more than 20 years. I ended up in a wheelchair, which I since have gotten myself out of. So the longer you delay healing the worse this can get. The good news is that you can do something about this yourself and you've already taken the first step in that direction by reading this book.

In light of all of this, we then would also need to consider trauma that we may have experienced early in our lives. Now that we have an understanding of how chronic stress/trauma can lead to future health problems, one would think this would be exacerbated even more by being preceded by early childhood trauma. Yes, to a certain extent this can lead to future illnesses like depression or personality disorders. However, early trauma may also have a positive effect on how we handle trauma as adults. Childhood trauma can lead to future problems, it also can have a positive side in the sense that in adulthood a person handles difficult situations in a better way. Adults who were stressed can also pass that coping behavior on to their children genetically.

This information caused me to reflect back on my own childhood. I experienced quite a bit of trauma as a child. I was picked on and beat up daily in school. My parents divorced when I was young. On top of getting beat up every day I also was told I was an a-hole constantly. I used to get yelled and screamed at and told I was stupid and didn't know what I was talking about on a daily basis. I always felt alone and abandoned. I was afraid to go to school and then I was afraid to go home. That negativity even carried on into my adulthood. Yes, that all did have a negative impact on my life. Sometimes, even to this day. However, at the same time, I can't help but think that it did have some positive effect on me. I learned how to cope with all of that and survive. I learned how to focus on certain things and not on others. That all influenced decisions I made in my life concerning my future, which all lead me to where I am today.

I made it through boot camp, the Marines, and combat. I suffered from PTS for more than 20 years. While that was going on I put myself through college, got a very good job as an archaeologist, and even purchased two homes. I eventually lost all of that, filed bankruptcy, contemplated ending my life twice, ended up in the hospital twice and I was put on five different medications, which all culminated in me being in a wheelchair for two years and gaining 80lbs.

I again had to recall my life experiences and use them to fix what was going on. I got fed up. I knew I could beat this, I knew I could survive. I had done it before many times since I was a child. I used those experiences to motivate me to force myself out of my wheelchair and subsequently quit all five of the medications I was on cold turkey. I made a new plan to rebuild my life. I focused on that instead of what I was suffering through and I enacted my plan. I wouldn't say that I have completed my plan as my plan spans an entire lifetime. However, I am well on my way and here I am telling the world about it. My point being, bad things happen and so do good. However, it all has a purpose and so do you and that's what you need to focus on. It's all about the focus, which I learned from all of my experiences that were good and especially the ones that were bad.

I would like to quote a passage from Paulo Coelho's book, Warrior of the Light. It is a passage he quoted from John Bunyan. It sums this all up quite well.

"Although I have been through all that I have, I do not regret the many hardships I met, because it was they who brought me to the place I wished to reach. Now all I have is this sword and I give it to whoever wishes to continue his pilgrimage. I carry with me the marks and scars of battles-they are the witnesses of what I suffered and the rewards of what I conquered. These are the beloved marks and scars that will open the gates of Paradise to me. There was a time when I used to listen to tales of bravery. There was a time when I lived only because I needed to live. But now I live because I am a Warrior and because I wish one day to be in the company of Him for whom I have fought so hard."

There are people whom are more resilient than others. Some people just have this ability to keep going no matter what and not give up even though they may be overwhelmed. Stress during childhood could actually be a good thing if the child can develop a mastery over the experience without being over protected by their parents. I myself growing up as a child in Detroit had to face a lot of hardships like bullying, etc. It did affect me, but not just in bad ways. It really has enabled me to overcome a lot of things. I had to learn to rely on past experiences in order to survive because I really didn't have anywhere else to turn. So, because I had these experiences, even though they were perceived as bad, I was able to overcome things. It's a practice that I continue to use even to this day. What this is really, is taking a negative experience and turning it into a positive one. As I remembered these events I told myself I have to learn how to use this to my advantage. These memories had negative emotions attached to them. However, because of what I used them for, they now also had positive emotions attached to them and that's what I chose to focus on.

Social support is also a key factor. It's like someone having your back in the sense that it helps motivate you to become more resilient. What this is really, is the individual thinking that because someone has their back they now have a purpose. This, in my opinion, is key. Having a purpose can be very motivating. That is why you must find your purpose in life and move towards that goal. Even if you don't have a person in your life, you must realize that you still have a purpose in the grander scheme of things. If you follow your path in life all other things that you require in order to achieve that purpose tend to fall into place, or be provided for you. I realize this seems a little esoteric, but it is very true.

Another key factor in resilience is exercise. Exercise can provide several benefits that are associated with resilience, such as improving mood, cognition and enhancing molecules that help repair cells damaged by stress. I know that in my own life running and/or hiking always help me to deal with stress. I actually work things out in my mind while exercising. I use that negative energy during the exercise and when I am done that negativity is gone. The more often that I do exercise, the stronger I feel both physically and mentally.

Another big factor in resilience, which I am a big proponent of, is mindfulness. Meditation has allowed people in horrible situations, such as POW's, to take themselves away from what is happening. In other words, it's an escape and a healthy one indeed. Another aspect of this is positivity. It can affect how an individual deals with something like PTS. This can be found in our police officers. By applying a positive attitude, having gratefulness for what they do have and being able to leave each situation at work, they are able to have long, successful careers. Sometimes, without ever having any incident of mental illness. Some people just have a higher resiliency than others. However, resiliency is obviously something that can be built by anyone. We can conduct self-healing processes that can prevent the development of PTS and other stress induced mental illnesses.

We previously discussed how your brain reacts to stress, stimuli and how it then re-records everything in your environment when the memory is triggered again in the future. We then also talked about how you must begin to retrain your brain with positive actions, such as I did in my bedroom when I was dealing with the issues I had with the color orange. Not only does retraining your brain with positive actions help to build your resiliency, but also having a positive attitude increases that greatly. By positive attitude I mean thinking to yourself that this experience will only make you stronger, or that you know in every bad situation there is always something which can be learned and applied to your life in a positive way. Hence, making you even stronger. This basically is the crux of resiliency.

Resilience is built by going through these types of traumatic experiences over and over again. However the "building" of this resiliency is highly dependent upon how the individual conducts him or herself after the event occurs. What I am talking about here is taking the time to identify that something has happened and that it was bad for you. Then you must process those emotions and release them by doing something like writing a letter about it and releasing it by crumbling the letter up and throwing it in the garbage. While doing this say to yourself, "I release you from my life." Follow this up with some gratitude for what you actually do have in your life. Then there needs to be a positive shift in your thinking, such as learning something positive from this experience and applying it to your life as you move forward with it. Thereby building a strong foundation (i.e., resiliency).

"Ok just a little pin prick. There'll be no more aaaaah! But you may feel a little sick. Can you stand up? I do believe it's working, good. That'll keep you going through the show. Come on its time to go. There is no pain, you are receding. A distant ship, smoke on the horizon. You are only coming through in waves. Your lips move but I can't hear what you're saying. When I was a child I caught a fleeting glimpse out of the corner of my eye. I turned to look but it was gone. I cannot put my finger on it now. The child is grown. The dream is gone. I have become comfortably numb."

Pink Floyd-Comfortably Numb

MEDICATIONS AND DRUGS

CHAPTER 4

It seems, as we have discussed, the main form of treatment the medical community uses for treating PTS is drugs. Quite often, the Veterans themselves turn to non-prescription drugs such as alcohol and/or marijuana in order to self-treat their PTS. These drugs obviously only exacerbate the problem and have accelerated the number of deaths related to PTS into epic proportions, because of this they have even put that on a schedule to become even more prolific.

Like I stated in a previous chapter, more Veterans are dying from suicide linked to PTS than are getting killed in the current Iraq and Afghanistan wars. These medications and drugs are only accelerating the problem. Yet doctors keep prescribing copious amounts of them to our Veterans and people in general.

All that these medications really do is numb you. They block a natural process that occurs in your body from happening. So when you get off of the medications, your problem returns. Or if you have been on them too long, your problems become worse and you then have to take more. Thereby facilitating dependency, drug abuse, health problems and quite often death.

It isn't until you become aware of yourself, your problems and try to ascertain why they are happening that you will actually begin to get better. You have to re-train your brain and hence, yourself. We do this in healthy, natural ways. You have to study your life and learn from it.

It appears that the medical community, our government and the VA are trying to extinguish the problem of PTS with drugs instead of actually trying to teach people how to heal from this debilitating and life threatening condition. All this is doing really, is making the situation worse.

Dr. Peter Breggin, a psychiatrist, testified before Congress about this issue of over drugging our troops. An analysis was conducted in 2012 by the Austin American-Statesman. Every drug purchase made by the DOD from the beginning of the second Gulf War until 2012 was looked at. He found that spending on drugs soared to 123% and spending had risen from $3 billion to $6.8 billion. This was double the increase in sales of pharmaceuticals in general in the U.S. Just on anti-depressants the military spent $2.7 billion for a decade after 9/11. In 2013 CBS acquired data from the VA that showed their patients increased 29%; however, their narcotics prescriptions were up a whopping 259%!

They are now saying that these psychiatric drugs are being prescribed to our troops before they even go on deployment and are not allowed to go unless they accept the drugs. Nurses have reported finding our Veterans are on three or four types of drugs already once they return home from a deployment.

The fact that the DOD, the military and the VA appear to be not only increasing the amounts of medications they are giving, but now giving them to troops before they go on deployment is a very scary progression. As we discussed in the first Chapter, these doctors and agencies even admit that these medications are bad for an individual, can increase the symptoms of PTS and in some cases these medications have been removed from their list of effective medicines.

While all of this continues to occur, the suicide rate of Veterans is at an all-time epidemic high level. Yet they just keep pumping our Veterans up with these dangerous psychotropic drugs. Drugs are not the answer to curing PTS. The drugs don't do anything for you. You have to learn coping skills and how to take care of yourself. Once you get off these drugs your problems will return unless you have acquired these skills. This is what these doctors should be teaching their patients. Furthermore, the longer you stay on the drugs the chance of them making your condition worse can increase, thereby leading to more types of and higher doses of drugs, which then lead to addiction. All of this information in combination with the fact that our government and the military keep prescribing these medications like a Pez dispenser should be a big warning signal to everyone. Especially, our troops and Veterans.

Depression has been linked to low serotonin levels. The most common type of medicine given to patients with depression are the Selective Serotonin Re-Uptake Inhibitors (SSRI's). They work by increasing the amount of serotonin produced by the brain. They are finding that these medications are actually making patients worse because they are interfering with the brain's natural recovery mechanism.

What people fail to realize is that most forms of depression, which can be painful, are actually natural and can have beneficial adaptations to stress. If the depressed person can realize that they are depressed, contemplate why they may be in that state and then take something positive out of it, they are building a foundation from which to cope with depression and stress effectively. A person must learn from their experiences by reflecting upon them. This then would obviously be a natural and very beneficial adaption to stress.

One of the definitive books written recently on mental health by Glenn R. Schiraldi, Ph.D. in 2009 is titled, "The Post-Traumatic Stress Disorder Sourcebook, Second Edition." It contains a very apropos quote from Dr. George Everly, "I've never seen anyone cured of PTSD with a pill."

Psychotropic medicines are supposed to be used to lessen certain symptoms of PTS. However, as we have been discussing, it seems they are being solely used to cure it.

All of these drugs have side effects and none of them will cure the problem. None of these drugs work effectively to cure guilt, grief, interpersonal difficulties and moral outrage, which are all symptoms of someone who has PTS! However, these medications may help to reduce re-occurring things such as nightmares, flashbacks, insomnia and/or irritability.

I will list below the types of medications and their specific names Dr. Schiraldi lists in his book, which are typically prescribed to patients with PTS and other mental conditions.

1. **Antidepressants:** Used for depression, anxiety and chronic pain. These types of medicines have a low risk of dependence.
    *SSRI'S (These prevent your brain from re-absorbing serotonin. Thereby changing the balance of serotonin

which seems to help brain cells send and receive chemical messages [Mayo Clinic 2013])
- Zoloft
- Paxil
- Fluoxetine (Prozac)
- Citalopram (Celexa)
- Escitalopram (Lexapro)

*Dual Action Antidepressants (These block serotonin and norepinephrine)
- Venlafaxine (Effexor)
- Duloxetine (Cymbalta)

*Monomine Oxidase Inhibitors (MAOI'S) (These were the 1st class of Antidepressants developed. They elevate levels of norepinephrine, Serotonin and dopamine. They have serious side effects if dietary restrictions are not followed and thus have been abandoned.)
- Phenelzine (Nordil)

*Tricyclics (These also elevate levels of norepinephrine and serotonin. However, they also block the action of acetylcholine. These have precautions that must be followed or they can lead to overdosing and interactions with SSRI's.)
- Imipramine (Tofranil)
- Amitriptyline (Elavil)

2. **Mood Stabilizers/Atypical Antipsychotic Agents:** These are not as often used but can be used when antidepressants do not work or to augment them. They can help with mood swings, rage, aggression, hypervigilance and hallucinations.

   *Atypical Antipsychotics
   - Risperdone (Risperdal)
   - Olanzapine (Zyprexa)
   - Quetiapine (Seroquel) [also helps with sleep]

*Mood Stabilizers
- Lithium (Eskalith)
- Carbamazepine (Tegretol)
- Divalproex (Depakote)

3. **Antiadrenergic Agents:** These are high blood pressure medications which block the actions of stress hormones in your body. They can also enhance the prefrontal cortical function of your brain.
   *Beta Blockers (Can block stress hormones which give traumatic memories their emotional charge. It is believed that these may help prevent PTSD if given before, or shortly after a traumatic event. Also can work to lessen a memories emotional intensity if taken after the memory occurs.
   - Propranolol (Inderal)

   *Alpha Blockers (Given for sleep and nightmares)
   - Prazosin (Minipres)
   - Clonidine (Catapres) [Helps with arousal and angry outbursts]

4. **D-Cycloserine** (Seromycin): Used for Tuberculosis but may reduce PTSD and augment prolonged exposure (PE).

5. **Benzodiazepines** (Anti-anxiety drugs/tranquilizers): Can quickly lessen anxiety but these are controversial and not recommended. These are very addictive and have complicated withdrawal symptoms. You can relapse when you quit using these. These medications can actually induce depression!
   - Diazepam (Valium)
   - Lorazepam (Ativan)
   - Alprazolam (Xanax)
   - Clonazepam (Klonopin)

6. **Buspirone** (BuSpar): Not a benzodiazepine but helps reduce arousal and has less dependence and withdrawals.

In general, all of these medications can have side effects such as dry mouth, dizziness, constipation, sleepiness and nervousness. They usually take 6-12 weeks to start working. If they haven't worked by then your doctor may increase your dosages, add other types, or change your medication(s) altogether. It may take a year or longer for a person to become stabilized on these medications.

Also, these meds can interact with other non-prescription drugs, alcohol and even things such as caffeine. Furthermore, these medications are designed to be used in conjunction with psychotherapy and not as the sole treatment for PTS. Once a person discontinues the medications their symptoms will return if they have not learned the proper skills necessary to overcome the PTS. It is recommended that an individual not quit all of their medications at once. They should be tapered down otherwise a relapse can occur as well as other things like sleep disruption, nausea or confusion.

Finally, you must eat a well-balanced meal including protein while on these medications. Some anti-depressants do not work well when certain things are missing from a person's diet, such as protein. Psychotherapy is usually considered more effective than the medications and when they are used together, they are thought of as the most beneficial.

The medical communities' focus seems to be all on medications. We now know that medications are the least effective of treatments unless they are used in conjunction with proper therapy. We also know when these medications are discontinued, or when the effects of them wear off, the symptoms of PTS usually return. We also know that the drug companies market their medications from the top down to such agencies as the DOD, the military and the VA whom can all profit monetarily from prescribing these drugs.

It seems as though treatment of war trauma has changed from listening to the Veteran's experiences into providing them with a quick fix in the form of a pill. It also appears to be evident that diagnosing PTS has spread to not only combat Veterans, but other Veterans whom never have seen combat. What this allows is the possibility to expand the numbers of people that they can prescribe these drugs to, which will then in turn allow them to make more money off of them at our Veterans expense.

Below is a list of several more deplorable facts from the Citizens Commission on Human Rights website www.cchr.org

- From 2001 to 2009, the Army's suicide rate increased more than 150% while orders for psychiatric drugs rose 76% over the same period.

- 85% of military suicide victims during that period had never even seen combat.

- With antidepressants, there are now nearly 100 drug regulatory agency warnings from ten countries and the European Union alerting prescribers and patients to the drugs adverse effects, including hostility, violent behavior and suicide.

- The U.S. DOD and the VA have spent almost $2 billion since 2001 to treat mental disorders.

- Every year the Australian Department of Veteran Affairs spends $160 million on mental health for its veterans.

- More British soldiers and veterans committed suicide in 2012 than were killed in battle.

- Between 2001 and 2009, there were 2,100 suicides in the U.S. military, triple the number of troops that died in Afghanistan and half of all American deaths in Iraq. During that same period, military orders for psychiatric drugs known to cause suicidal thoughts and acts increased 76%!

- Between 2005 and 2011, the rate of antipsychotic drug use in the U.S. military rose 1,100%! Far exceeding comparable rates in the civilian population.

- Seven different countries as well as the European Union have issued a total of 55 warnings about the harmful side effects of antipsychotic drugs, including:
    o 12 warnings of death/sudden death
    o 11 warnings of heart problems
    o 6 warnings of withdrawal symptoms
    o 6 warnings of convulsions, seizures or tremors
    o 5 warnings of diabetes

- Neurologist Dr. Fred Baughman, Jr., as many as 351 soldiers have died from cardiac arrest after ingesting drug cocktails containing antipsychotics and antidepressants.

- Between 2001 and 2011, the U.S. VA and Defense Department spent more than $850 million on Seroquel (this is sometimes referred to as Sero-Kill).

- In 1945, a leading international psychiatrist, British Brigadier General John Rawlings Rees, saw the military as psychiatry's perfect research lab. He stated, "The army and the other fighting services form rather unique experimental groups since they are complete communities, and it is possible to arrange experiments in a way that would be very difficult in civilian life."

- From the 1950's through the 1970's, psychiatrists in countries like Britain, the U.S. and the USSR used their militaries as proving grounds for an arsenal of new experimental treatments such as LSD. The U.S. Army estimated that at least 1,500 soldiers were given LSD as part of mind control experiments during this era.

What this exemplifies is that we are seeing some trends emerging here. The first one is that they are more easily diagnosing people with PTS. The second is that they are now also giving PTS medications to troops before they even go on deployment. The third is they are now adding existing medications that are used to treat other conditions to the treatment of PTS. All of this increases the number of people these drugs can be marketed to and increases the amounts and types of these medications that can be used to treat PTS. This would allow the possibility of increasing the profitability of such agencies as the VA, DOD, military and of course the drug companies.

Another thing has come to light lately. It's the use of medical marijuana to treat the symptoms of PTS. Wikipedia describes medical cannabis as follows: "Medical cannabis refers to the use of cannabis and its constituent cannabinoids, such as tetrahydrocannabinol (THC) and cannabidiol (CBD). In recent years the American Medical Association, the MMA, the American Society of Addiction Medicine, and other medical organizations have issued statements opposing its usage for medicinal purposes. Its use for other medical applications has been studied, but there is insufficient data for conclusions about safety and efficacy. Short term use increases minor adverse effects, but does not appear to increase major adverse effects. Long term effects of cannabis are not clear and there are safety concerns including memory and cognition problems and risk for dependence."

Long term exposure to cannabis can carry a risk of irreversible damage to a person's memory and intelligence if used as a child. Of the consumers who use cannabis on a daily basis, it has been stated that 20% of them become dependent. It is thought to be less addictive than cocaine or heroin, but more addictive than psilocybin, mescaline and LSD.

Cannabis can contribute to psychosis especially when it's used frequently and/or in higher doses. Exposure to it from an early age also increases the chance of developing psychosis. The two main ingredients of cannabis, THC and CBD do have opposing effects on each other. The THC is the ingredient that causes the adverse psychological effects and the CBD can counteract that. There is evidence which shows that cannabis use can worsen an individual's psychotic symptoms and increase their risk for a relapse. There was also an analysis conducted in 2014 which showed that there was an association between the use of cannabis and anxiety. It can also increase the risk of psychosis in individuals with certain genetic dispositions. It also can cause permanent psychological maladies in some users such as cognitive impairment, anxiety, paranoia, and increased risk of psychosis.

There is a relationship between early use and continued use of cannabis into adulthood and an increase in major depressive disorder (MOD) in an individual's adulthood. In users of all ages there is an increase in the risk of developing depression and heavy users have the highest risk. Cannabis may also worsen the frequency of manic type symptoms. Also, those who use cannabis into adulthood do show an increase in suicidal ideation and suicide attempts. Cannabis is a risk factor in suicidality, but there are also many other additional risk factors that contribute to it as well. It is believed that cannabis use leads to the use of other harder drugs.

As far as physical health is concerned, a 2013 literature review showed that cannabis use is associated with liver, lung, heart and vasculature disease. Cannabis use has been linked to bladder cancer and it contributes to the risk of head and neck cancer as well.

Marijuana use has been increasing in younger people since 2007. Also there are a few states whom have legalized recreational use of the drug and there are 21 states that have approved its use for medicinal purposes. This increase in usage is concomitant with the increase of prescriptions and usage of psychotropic drugs for PTS since the 2nd Gulf war in 2006. This is a very interesting correlation.

Marijuana can target specific molecules in the brain called cannabinoid receptors. These influence things such as pleasure, memory, thinking and time perception. It therefore also affects thinking, problem solving, learning and an individual's memory. It also affects brain development. A study in New Zealand studied people whom smoked marijuana between ages 13 and 38. They lost cognitive abilities and they were never fully restored when they quit smoking it as adults.

Marijuana smoke is irritating to the lungs and users can have the same respiratory problems as tobacco smokers. In fact, a study found that people who frequently smoked it have more health problems and miss more days of work than people who don't smoke it and most of their problems are related to respiratory issues.

Marijuana can also raise an individual's heart rate by 20-100% soon after smoking it. It has been estimated that people who use marijuana are 4.8 times more likely to have a heart attack within one hour of smoking the marijuana.

There have been many studies and several large ones which have linked chronic marijuana use to psychosis. Other factors which influenced this were genetics, amount of drug, drug potency and the age at which it was first taken. It also has been associated with other mental disorders such as depression, anxiety, suicidal thoughts and personality disturbances like lack of motivation.

The types of and dose strength of psychotropic medications have increased as well along with the amount of THC in marijuana. It has been revealed that contrary to many people's belief, marijuana is addictive. They say those who use it daily are 25-50% likely to become addicted. The withdrawal symptoms from cannabis are similar to the withdrawal symptoms of psychotropic medications used for PTS.

One can clearly see that not only is marijuana use detrimental to an individual's health, but it also can cause the same problems as the use of psychotropic medications, such as increased anxiety, psychosis, depression, etc. These problems are the very reason an individual is prescribed psychotropic drugs or medical marijuana in the first place. They actually can cause the problem to get worse especially with longer term use. The medical community knows this and has even stated that (as I have showed you) yet they still prescribe these drugs to patients for PTS and the types, strengths and amounts of these drugs are increasing along with an increased easiness of the diagnosis of PTS for individuals. The theme here is quite obvious. The DOD, military and the VA appear to be creating an epidemic of grand proportions, which also holds the possibility of profiting from it at the expense of our nation's military members and Veterans whom were so unselfishly willing to put their lives on the line for their country. Then they come home to get treated in this abusive manner by the very people they swore an allegiance to defend.

Panic attacks are a big part of having PTS. They come from and/or are precipitated by anxiety and paranoia, which the psychotropic drugs, marijuana and alcohol can also cause. At my worst I used to get them every day. At times, they would get so severe that I would pass out. I started trying to deal with them by self-medicating with alcohol. However, as we have discussed, this only made my panic attacks more severe. This caused me to drink even more thus creating a vicious cycle.

I then moved on to other archaic methods of dealing with them, such as putting a rubber band around my wrist and snapping it every time I got a panic attack in order to break the cycle. That worked for a bit. However, I then began to deal with this issue in more logical, natural, healthy ways.

There are several known panic attack symptoms. They are as follows:

- Pounding, racing heart
- Sweating
- Shaking
- Shortness of breath

- Choking sensation
- Chest discomfort
- Nausea
- Dizzy, feeling faint
- Feelings of unreality or detached from self
- Tingling or numbness
- Chills or heat sensations

It is important to note that panic attacks can mimic other symptoms, such as heart problems, respiratory problems, hormone problems, etc. So it is important to get checked out by a primary care doctor to evaluate if you have a real physical medical condition.

There are however, several relatively simple things that you can do for yourself in order to combat this devastating issue. The first thing, as with most cases, is education. First, try to educate yourself about the symptoms of a panic attack. Once you know what they are, it is much easier to identify them and begin to deal with the problem.

Secondly, try to understand how your brain works when it tries to process fear, such as the amygdala can misfire producing a sudden increase in adrenaline which can then lead to a panic attack. Once you understand that there is a perfectly logical explanation for that, you can then begin to tell yourself this when you're having the panic attack in order to help calm you down. For instance, when I used to get them, say in the grocery store checkout line, I would repeat to myself over and over again that I understood that this was a logical response to perceived fear and it was happening because I was in line and felt trapped. Then I would tell myself everything is ok. I am just buying groceries so I can just calm down now. After practicing this numerous times it began to work quite well for me.

The next thing you can do is too slow down your breathing. When you panic, you will breathe quite rapidly. This can cause you to hyperventilate. Just slow down your breathing by taking long deep breaths through your nose deep into your lungs and then exhaling through your mouth slowly. I still do this when I go to bed at night. I repeat it four or five times and then I am calm enough to fall asleep. Even dogs do this. If you notice when they lay down to sleep they always take a deep breath and then exhale and they fall asleep. Their hearts beat a lot faster than ours, so if it can work for a dog, it can work for you.

After slowing my breathing I then begin to relax my body. I do this by tensing my muscles up and releasing them as I inhale and exhale. I begin with my toes and work my way up to my head. As I release my muscles I try to pay attention to the feeling I get, such as my heart beating, my blood pumping through my extremities and feeling the tingling in my muscles. This is really quite relaxing. I even do this when I meditate.

Then, the other important factors are doing things such as eating a healthy diet and exercising. Neglecting your health can not only cause panic attacks, but also bring on your PTS among other health issues. There are also many other alternative things you can do, such as yoga, meditation, massage, herbs and supplements instead of resorting to medications and drugs. We will be spending the next chapter discussing all of these things in detail. In general, it is my opinion that medication should only be used as a last resort, whether prescription or not, if all other natural, healthy alternatives have failed.

"Without mental health there can be no true physical health."

Dr. Brock Chisholm, Director-General of the World Health Organisation, 1954.

HEALTHY, NATURAL PTS TIPS

CHAPTER 5

In this next chapter I want to discuss the plethora of information which is out there on nutritional, healthy things you can do for yourself that help you deal with PTS and eventually overcome it. With these things you will be building the foundation to begin retraining your brain and to lead healthy rewarding lives. We will be discussing things such as nutrition, exercise, mindfulness, meditation, yoga, etc. Most of these things I practice myself. As with anything, it all takes practice and you need to adopt a schedule for these things to be effective. Don't expect to be cured in one day. It takes time but you can do it.

It's true that the memories of your trauma may never completely disappear. However, you can certainly take away the emotional charge of these memories, which is what actually controls your life and causes the anxiety. In other words they just become memories and you render those memories powerless.

There a four general things you need to do in order to overcome your PTS. The first one is to reach out to others for support. I realize this may be difficult because as a part of your PTS you are probably avoiding everyone and everything. You may have even lost your family and friends altogether as I did. However, it is very important that you stay connected in order to defeat your feelings of isolation.

You can simply start by just talking to people in your community like the postal worker, the local store clerk, etc. Check in with family members from time to time. Also, stay connected with the world by reading the paper or watching the news. You can also stay connected through pets, such as a dog or a cat. You can volunteer at your local animal shelter or a ranch and start a friendship with an animal. They can be very loyal and wonderful friends whom never pass judgement. That's why they have animals such as working dogs who help Veterans with PTS.

The second thing is to avoid alcohol and drugs. The use of these drugs are only going to make things worse. They may have a very temporary effect, but they will make the symptoms of your PTS worse and cause future health problems that may not be reversible. Plus they can cause relationship problems and interfere with your job, etc.

The third general thing to do is to challenge your sense of helplessness. PTS is very overwhelming and powerful and can leave you feeling like there is absolutely nothing you can do about it. But you have to fight this. You have to take back what was taken from you. You must remember that you do have strengths and coping skills. Everyone and everything does and the ones you don't know, you can learn and apply. One of the best ways to do this is by helping and/or teaching others. This is also the best way to learn. By taking these types of actions you directly challenge your sense of helplessness and the more you do it, the more you learn and the more confident you become.

The fourth thing to do is to try and spend time in nature. This did wonders for me. I still do it today when I get stressed out. The outdoors provides you a place to be without all of the distractions of everyday life. It's a place where you can get good clean oxygen, clean out your mind and really begin to focus on what's important. Nature is a good example of the cycle of life. Find a nice spot outdoors. Then just sit, be still and observe. You will see that things are born and things expire. But what becomes evident is that while this cycle repeats itself, the energy within you and everything else on this planet is constant and never ending. It is always omnipresent. This you will find very comforting and you will realize that while material things come and go, life continues in perpetuity.

There are also a few steps you can take to help a loved one who has PTS.

*Be as patient as possible. Understand that healing takes time, effort and support.

*Try to anticipate possible PTS triggers and prepare for them accordingly.

*Remember to not take the symptoms of PTS personally. The PTS may have nothing to do with you or your relationship with the individual.

*Don't push your loved one into talking. Typically they will only do it when they feel they are ready. Accept that, but try to let them know that you are there for them when they finally do decide to open up.

There are a lot of natural and herbal supplements on the market today. These supplements can cause interactions with certain medications so make sure you talk to your doctor before trying any of these supplements. However, some of the more general ones that may help with PTS are St. John's wort, ginkgo biloba, passion flower, rhodiola (or roseroot) and valerian. There are also two amino acids that are said to be effective in treating anxiety. They are L-glutamine and L-histidine and they help by reducing stress and irritability. There also is the amino acid GABA. It supposedly can affect your brain in relation to your anxiety. Finally, there are two naturally occurring compounds, 5-HTP and SAMe, both of which have been shown to be just as effective as many of the prescription antidepressants that are on the market today.

The next thing I want to mention is exercise. This is very important and highly effective. It was one of the best things I ever did to help my PTS. You don't have to go nuts with this. You don't have to go out and try and run a marathon or bench press 500 pounds, or try and make the Olympic team, unless that is your own personal goal and that is what makes you happy. You simply just need to incorporate some form of exercise in your daily routine. When I started doing this 20 years ago I ran. I would just run two miles every day. Nothing major. It was something manageable that I could get myself to do every day. It worked. It by itself did not completely treat my PTS, but it was an important part of my healing. The exercise made me feel good physically and it also made me feel good mentally because by accomplishing that goal every day it built my confidence. It also forced me to eat right and take care of myself so that I could perform properly. Plus exercise is known to release endorphins into your body that help you to feel better. It also helped because while I was exercising I was getting copious amounts of fresh air and quite often whatever problem I had at the time, I worked it out while I was running. I used that negative energy in my running thereby turning a negative into a positive and when I was done exercising I had burnt off all of that negativity. I still exercise today. Albeit, not as much as

I would like, but I still do. I walk my dog every day for about 20 to 30 minutes and just that little bit of exercise always alleviates my stress. I try to go hiking whenever I can. This really works well. Any time I have any major problems or have to make big decisions, I work them out while I am hiking. I arm myself with as much knowledge as possible and then I think about it while I hike without all of the distractions of everyday life. I can truly focus and concentrate solely on my issues at hand. The other big thing exercise did for me was that it improved the quality of my sleep. That is huge. Anyone who has PTS knows that quality sleep is hard to come by let alone if you can sleep at all. What is evident here is that without proper mental health there really is no true physical health and obviously exercise appears to be directly relevant to both. You can definitely help yourself accomplish this by exercising as I just mentioned. This will be one of the best things you can do for yourself. Not only for overcoming your PTS, but to be successful in life itself!

Diet is probably the very best thing you can do for yourself. There is a plethora of information on eating a healthy diet. If you take care of your brain, your brain will take care of you. If your brain is not functioning properly, how can the rest of your body work properly? It controls everything. But, before I discuss diet, I want to discuss cortisol as it is produced in response to stress like I mentioned before. The buildup of cortisol in your body over an extended period of time can cause several types of health problems. Your diet can help you remove cortisol from your body and help you to reduce stress as you will have better control over your brain, which in turn will be less inclined to produce the cortisol in the first place.

Wikipedia states that as a response to stress and low blood glucose, your brain produces cortisol and that cortisol has several primary functions such as increasing blood sugar, suppressing the immune system, aids in the metabolism of fat, protein and carbohydrate and it also decreases bone formation. It also states that cortisol can cause many other specific health problems. I have provided a paraphrased list of those for you below:

* Weakens the activity of the immune system.
* Affects the body's natural killer cells.
* Reduces bone formation.
* Reduces calcium absorption in the intestine
* Inhibits collagen (collagen loss in the skin is 10 times greater than in any other tissue).
* Lengthens wound healing time.
* Counteracts insulin, contributes to hyperglycemia.
* Decreases amino acid intake by muscle and inhibits protein synthesis.
* Stimulates gastric-acid secretion.
* Acts as an antidiuretic hormone controlling one-half of intestinal diuresis.
* Inhibits sodium loss through the small intestine of mammals.
* Causes intense potassium excretion.
* Works with adrenaline to create memories of short-term emotional events.
* Increases blood pressure.
* Causes kidneys to produce hypotonic urine. (When dehydration results in a decreased sodium concentration, which suggests the cause of dehydration and must be treated with great caution to avoid severe neurologic damage.)
* Shuts down the reproductive system.
* Reduces serotonin levels in the brain.
* There are potential links between cortisol, appetite and obesity.

Wikipedia also lists things that reduce and increase cortisol levels in the body. I have also provided those to you below:

Factors reducing cortisol
* Magnesium supplementation after aerobic exercise
* Omega-3 fatty acids

* Music therapy
* Massage therapy
* Laughing
* Black tea (hastens recovery from high cortisol conditions)
* Regular dancing

Factors increasing cortisol
* Viral infections
* Caffeine
* Sleep deprivation
* Intense or prolonged physical exercise
* Severe trauma or stressful events
* Anorexia nervosa
* Serotonin receptor gene 5HTR2C associated with increased cortisol production in men.
* Severe calorie restriction
* Continuous consumption of alcohol for an extended period of time.

Now, I don't know about you but out of all of the doctors I saw for PTS not a single one of them recommended any of this to me to try. They just went right to the hard core psychotropic drugs. Secondly, you would think the military would make sure that you ate very well, especially while you were deployed. When I was in Saudi Arabia our food was horrible. I had food poisoning twice and dysentery for three months. We got one MRE to eat a day. We never got any nutritional supplements either. I would send letters home asking for food. When I went to Saudi Arabia I weighed 170lbs and was in the best shape of my life. When I came home, I weighed 140lbs, had holes in my teeth big enough to stick my tongue in, smoked like a chimney, and had been exposed to nasty toxins, chemical warfare and we had non FDA approved drugs tested on us.

Now, back to your diet. Obviously, the first thing you want to do with your diet is to start eating things that will help you reduce the cortisol levels in your body. Just as with anything else, if you eat a well-balanced diet, you generally will be in good health. I will now discuss several different things that you can add to your diet that were not mentioned in the Wikipedia article. These things also will generally make you healthier over all. So, it's a win win situation.

Vitamin D and omega-3 fatty acid are two very important things that are obtained easily that can help you overcome your PTS. They help the brain to function and they affect the way we behave. Vitamin D may control serotonin, which can affect your behavior and also psychiatric disorders. You can get vitamin D by going out in the sun or just drink a glass of milk. Omega 3 fatty acid is also good for heart health and it contains anti-inflammatory properties. For omega-3 all you have to do is eat fish a couple times a week. Or, if you don't like fish, you can take supplements. They even make them so you won't get a fishy after taste. They work well. I know. I have some at home that I take when I can't get good fish at the store.

Another good source of omega fatty acids is olive oil. However, it must be extra virgin olive oil. Extra virgin is the only oil that contains all the antioxidants and bioactive compounds. I like the Greek extra virgin olive oil the best as it has a much less peppery bite to it. I take a tablespoon of olive oil every morning and I use it in all of my cooking and food preparation.

To take olive oil a little further, there are 11 known health benefits of olive oil. They are as follows:

*1 Rich in Monounsaturated fats (Oleic acid, which is linked to reduced inflammation and its beneficial effects on genes linked to cancer). Has a resistance to high heat which makes it great for cooking.

*2 Contains large amounts of antioxidants (such as vitamins A and K which are good for heart health, expansion of your arteries, aides against plaque formation and aides in preventing cancer).

*3 Strong anti-inflammatory properties (3.4 tablespoons of extra virgin olive oil has a similar effectiveness as 10% of an adult dose of ibuprofen).

*4 May help prevent a stroke

*5 Protective against heart disease (lowers inflammation, protects LDL cholesterol from oxidation, improves function of the lining of the blood vessels and may aide against unwanted blood clotting).

*6 Olive oil does not cause weight gain (eating fat does not make you fat. It is nutrient dense and keeps you feeling full longer so you eat less).

*7 May help fight Alzheimer's disease (see, it's good for your brain!).

*8 May reduce the risk of type 2 diabetes (has beneficial effects on blood sugar and insulin sensitivity. A Mediterranean diet with olive oil reduced risk of type 2 diabetes by over 40%.)

*9 Anti-oxidants in olive oil have anti-cancer properties.

*10 Can help treat Rheumatoid arthritis (reduces joint pain and swelling from rheumatoid arthritis).

*11 Has anti-bacterial properties (studies have shown extra virgin olive oil to be effective against eight strains of bacteria, three of which are resistant to antibiotics).

The next thing I want to mention is protein. If you recall, when we discussed cortisol I mentioned that one of the primary effects of increased cortisol levels in the body was the metabolism of protein. Protein is extremely important for your body and it is very nutrient dense as is fat. So, when you are stressed and producing elevated levels of cortisol you begin to metabolize protein. Therefore, you need to make sure that you get enough protein in your diet.

There is a particular diet that comes to mind which includes olive oil in it. It is called the Mediterranean diet. This diet (high in olive oil) can have health benefits for your brain even to the point that it can cut the risk of Alzheimer's and can counter the effects of aging on the brain, not to mention the benefits of cardiovascular health. The diet basically consists of olive oil, nuts, unrefined grains, beans, berries (blueberries), green leafy vegetables, fish and wine. In some cases this diet has shown some benefits in memory function and processing.

Now that we've talked about fat and protein, lets discuss herbs and spices. Here is a list of 10 herbs and spices that may help you reduce the effects of chronic stress and cortisol on your body.

*1 Cinnamon, which can lower blood sugar levels and contains an anti-diabetic effect.

*2 Sage. It may help improve brain function and memory.

*3 Peppermint. This can help with Irritable Bowel Syndrome (IBS) pain and may even reduce nausea.

*4 Turmeric (contains curcumin) which is known to have anti-inflammatory and antioxidant (curcumin) properties.

*5 Holy basil can aid in the fight against bacterial infections and boost your immunity.

*6 Cayenne pepper helps to reduce your appetite and is said to have anti-cancer properties.

*7 Ginger eases nausea and also contains anti-inflammatory properties.

*8 Fenugreek can improve glucose metabolism.

*9 Rosemary is said to prevent allergies and nasal congestion.

*10 Garlic fights sickness and improves your heart health.

Another interesting and important food source is Spirulina. I take Spirulina daily in tablet form. In case you don't know, Spirulina is a naturally growing blue, green algae and it contains many nutrients. Because of this, and the fact that I take other supplements and I eat healthy, I only take half of the recommended dosage. It does great things for me health and energy wise and I am a big proponent of it. Below is a list of the 10 known benefits of spirulina.

*1 Spirulina is very high in many nutrients, such as protein, vitamins B1, B2, B3, B12, copper, iron, vitamin A, magnesium, potassium and manganese and small amounts of almost every other nutrient that we need.

*2 Contains powerful antioxidants and anti-inflammatory properties.

*3 Can lower your LDL and Triglyceride levels.

*4 Protects LDL cholesterol from becoming oxidized.

*5 May have anti-cancer properties, especially against oral cancer.

*6 Said to reduce blood pressure.

*7 May improve symptoms of allergic rhinitis.

*8 May effect anemia in a positive way

*9 Can increase muscle strength and endurance.

*10 May help you control your blood sugar.

Now that we have discussed all of these healthy supplements, herbs, spices, food, etc., I want to discuss a particular diet with you that I follow, which goes a step further than the Mediterranean diet we previously discussed. This diet will not only cover what we just discussed about naturally healing your PTS, but it also has many other overall health benefits such as preventing arthritis, cancer, heart disease, bone loss, and dental cavities. All of which are related to having, and/or caused from, PTS if it is left untreated.

As we discussed, PTS causes the body to produce cortisol which can cause many of the health problems I just mentioned in the previous paragraph. Prescription medications, drugs (such as cannabis) and alcohol only exacerbate this problem immensely. So, we must lower the cortisol levels in our bodies and eliminate the toxins in order to move forward. You can do this in healthy, natural ways.

First of all, we begin with our diet and the elimination of "bad" things we put/have put into our bodies. These "toxins" (as I like to call them) can actually block your body from absorbing the proper nutrients and/or cause you to excrete them from your body before you can utilize them. Take alcohol for instance, it can cause you to excrete vitamin A among other things. One of the more notable symptoms of this is blurry vision. This happened to me. Once I eliminated the alcohol and other toxins, ate healthy and took natural supplements my blurry vision cleared up within days.

As far as meat, vegetables, dairy, supplements and water goes, always remember natural/organic is the best. Otherwise, those things are loaded with antibiotics, GMO's and other horrible chemicals not to mention the nasty fertilizers things are grown with. So, when you shop always look for organic/grass fed products without these toxins. With some products you will not be able to help but buy the toxin filled products, but the more you eliminate from your diet the better off you will be. You will be able to find most of these things at your local farmers market or stores like Sprouts, Trader Joe's, Whole Foods, etc. Most things in moderation will not harm you as long as you get the proper nutrition.

First, my diet consists of meat (with the bone in), fish, eggs and dairy. Again, with all of these go with the organic, grass fed products. I even buy organic, grass fed butter. It is way better than any other butter. I am lactose intolerant so dairy can be a problem. However, I buy raw, organic goats milk. I can drink it all day long without any problems at all. Its natural, unrefined and more easily digestible, has less sugar and is much healthier for you than store bought milk. It even contains vitamin A and C! The reason you want meat with the bone in is because you will take the bones and boil them with vegetables to make a broth that contains all of the gelatin, essential oils and fats that your body needs. This broth is what I usually have for lunch. There is a myth out there that fat is bad for you and that eating fat causes you to get fat. This is entirely not true. If you don't believe me look it up. Fat is nutrient dense and keeps you feeling full longer so you eat less, which causes you to lose weight not gain it. Also, fat is necessary for the absorption and transportation of several important vitamins. This leads us to the next step of our diet, necessary fat soluble vitamins.

Your body must have vitamins A, D (especially D3), E, and K (especially K2). These vitamins are all fat soluble. They need fat in order to be absorbed and transported by your body. It's simple. No fat, no vitamins. When I was an archaeologist, I studied humans that lived 25,000 years ago. When they would kill an animal, there were several things they ate right away. They were the heart, liver, tongue and FAT. All of these are extremely nutrient rich.

Now, there are two forms of vitamin A. One is Retinol which comes from animal products and the second are Carotenoids like beta carotene, which come from vegetables such as green and yellow ones and carrots. We get most of our vitamin A from vegetables. A person can develop toxicity from vitamin A, but that's usually with the Retinol type.

Vitamin E has two forms when you buy the supplements from the store. There is a natural one called alpha tocopheryl or D alpha tocopheryl. The synthetic one is dl alpha tocopheryl acetate. The acetate is a preservative. I try to stick with the natural vitamin E. There was a small study that stated the synthetic form increased prostate cancer in men, but they weren't sure of the correlation as they needed to study the vitamin E levels and selenium levels in the blood before they partook in the study. As with anything, natural is better.

Vitamin K (especially K2) helps you with blood clotting, heart disease, healthy skin, forming strong bones, promoting brain function, supporting growth and development and helping to prevent cancer. It also helps to expand your arteries for better blood flow. Vitamin D3 is good for heart and arterial health, healthy blood pressure and bone health. Too much can cause toxicity as well, but you would have to be taking quite a bit. As with any of this, do your research on the proper levels of vitamins you should take and consult your doctor, especially if you are taking medicine, before taking any supplements.

Next, you need to eat green leafy vegetables such as kale, spinach, water cress, bok choy and certain fruits like blue berries, raspberries and apples. Next you will also need to get calcium, phosphorous, magnesium and zinc. These all help with bone formation and health and you need them all in order to process them. For instance, you need phosphorous to properly utilize calcium, etc. You will get these vitamins and minerals from your green leafy vegetables, etc., but I also take supplements. These particular ones are usually taken at night because they also help repair cells and damaged muscle tissue while you sleep. This is why weight lifters often take magnesium. It is also necessary to get probiotics. Yogurt, apple cider vinegar and sauerkraut are good sources of these. In the morning before I eat I take a tablespoon of extra virgin olive oil and apple cider vinegar. Then after eating, I take my vitamins.

Finally, you want to eliminate refined sugars and starches from your diet. In particular, these can cause bacteria in your mouth that attract acids which cause tooth decay and prevent healthy antibacterial fluids in your mouth. You will also want to eliminate legumes, grains, nuts, and seeds from your diet. These all contain large amounts of phytic acid which causes vitamins and minerals to be leeched from your body and/or not utilized. For instance, phytic acid binds 80% of your phosphorous so you can't use it. You just excrete it. It also causes a 20% decrease in Zinc absorption and 60% decrease in magnesium absorption. So, just imagine what you are doing to your bones by eating this coupled with the fact that you have PTS which causes cortisol production which then can cause bone deformation. Starting to get the picture here? Now, you can eat these things in moderation if they come from sprouted grains and seeds. Another trick to reducing the phytic acid in these foods is to soak them yourself until they sprout or roast and salt them or eat them with vitamin C.

You may also be experiencing dental problems as a result of having PTS and your nutritional deficiencies. What you can do is make your own toothpaste with coconut oil, baking soda (without aluminum), peppermint oil and stevia. Secondly, every morning upon waking rinse your mouth for 20 minutes with a tablespoon of unrefined-virgin coconut oil, then rinse with warm salt water for extra purification and then floss and brush normally. What this actually does is remove the bacteria, toxins and mucous from not only your gums and teeth but from your system as well. You will notice your nose draining while you do this. Remember, your mouth is the beginning of your digestive process and parts of what you eat and drink (i.e., whatever you place in your mouth) gets absorbed quickly into your blood stream through the many capillaries (blood vessels) in your mouth and gums. I do these things every day and my teeth and gums have never felt and looked cleaner and I feel great.

Lastly, on the subject of diets and nutrition, there are a few things to remember. First of all, make sure you eat a well-balanced meal. Then you can add vitamin and mineral supplements. They should only be used to "top you off" and not as your only source of nutrition. You can get too much of a good thing and cause a toxicity in your system with vitamins and minerals. As with anything, everything in moderation. I will provide you with some general guidelines to follow and a few things that I do myself.

First of all, there are two types of vitamins, fat soluble and water soluble. The first are transported in fat through your system and then stored in your tissues. Therefore, these can build up over time and cause toxicity. Your fat soluble vitamins are A, D, E, and K. Now, most experts will say that a lot of the daily recommendations are below what we really need. Especially with vitamin D. Chronic stress produces cortisol and that will leach vitamins out of your system, especially vitamin A and more so vitamin D. A lack of vitamin D can make you more susceptible to diseases such as colds, flu and respiratory ailments. So, if you have PTS and you get these diseases frequently, this is probably why. Therefore, I am not as concerned about the amount of vitamin D I am getting as I am about vitamin A. I monitor how much vitamin A I get each day, especially the animal version (Retinol) like we discussed.

The water soluble vitamins are transported through water. Therefore, any excess of these you will simply pass through urination. Such vitamins are your B vitamins. There are eight of them, B6, B12, Folate, Niacin, Riboflavin, Thiamine, etc. So, it is very hard to get toxicity from B vitamins. The second type of vitamin A, Carotenoids, or Beta-carotene is water soluble as well.

Furthermore, certain vitamins and/or minerals will counteract each other and you will not absorb them properly, such as calcium will block iron. Zinc can also compete with iron absorption. However, vitamin C will counteract this blocking of iron by calcium. So, as a general rule, I try to consume vitamin C with most of my meals. For breakfast I make sure I have V8 juice which contains vitamin C and I do not consume any dairy products which are high in calcium. At lunch I have my dairy products in the form of a 4oz glass of raw goat's milk. At dinner I squeeze lemon juice on my salad and if I do not have salad, I squeeze lemon into my water to get my vitamin C. I usually have meat with dinner, which contains iron. Lastly, I take my calcium, magnesium, phosphorous and zinc supplements at night before bed with some food, such as yogurt for proper absorption of those minerals. Plus, those minerals help to repair damaged cells and tissues at night while you rest and I found they also help me to sleep. You can take them with your dinner also. I do this as well.

Keep in mind what I said about stress producing cortisol, which leaches vitamins and minerals from your system. So, you need to reduce your stress levels. B vitamins will help you do this along with all of the nutritional and physical things we have been talking about, such as exercise. B vitamins are good for your nerves, brain and overall well-being.

Finally, as with any diet or exercise program consult your primary care doctor and at the very least do your own research. It's very easy now a days since information is everywhere. Especially with computers, tablets and cellphones. Most of the information I have given you here is from personal research I have conducted. This is by no means a be all and end all list of things; however, it's a good place to start.

Now let's discuss a few other things you may do to improve not only your lifestyle, but your physical and mental health such as, yoga and meditation. I have never personally practiced yoga; however, I know several people who have and they say it works wonders for them. They say its great exercise and helps to balance your body and mind. I can see how this would work. I give you all of this information on different techniques and nutrition with the understanding that you will try some and not others. The idea behind this is that I am giving you everything that exists so you can then pick and choose what appeals to you and try it. So, try different things and stick to what works for you. That is what I do. The other aspect of this is meditation. This is something I practice religiously on a daily basis. It works for me. It's a way for me to escape the world and all of my problems. I usually do it at bed time because it relaxes me and helps me to sleep. It helps me to clear my conscious so that I may fall asleep without being kept awake by thoughts and things that I have been worrying about. Basically, it is MY peace time. Meditating this time of night also works well for me because a lot of times during the day we all get busy working and/or getting necessary things done like dinner, laundry, washing the car, shopping, etc. At bed time I don't have to worry about these things.

They say that one of the biggest benefits of yoga is becoming in tune with your body. This is what it is all about. When you become in tune with your body you will realize that your body will actually tell you when something is not right and conversely it will let you know when everything is great. Once you pick up on this you will then understand how to begin to heal what's wrong or concentrate on what is right. It's all about awareness, which is one of the most important first steps you must take in beginning your healing process. We will discuss that more in greater detail in the last chapter.

There are three simple yoga moves you can practice daily. They are: **1. Life nerve stretch**-Sit on floor with legs spread apart. Inhale and raise your arms up. Exhale and touch your foot. Repeat and touch the other foot. **2. Spinal flex**-Sit cross legged on the floor. Grab your shins and inhale and arch your back, bringing your chest forward. Exhale and round your back. **3. Shoulder shrugs**-Sit cross legged with hands on your knees. Inhale and raise shoulders. Exhale and lower your shoulders back down. Repeat each of these steps for one to three minutes. This all seems pretty simple and a good way to clear your mind and get in tune with your body for the day.

Meditation is also very powerful. Don't expect to get it right on your first attempt. This is something that does take a little practice, but it is definitely well worth the effort. Like I said, I like to meditate at night when I go to bed. However, when I get the chance I also do it during the day no matter where I am at. Here are a few easy things to try when you begin your practice of meditation. **Breathe**-Take slow, deep breaths. This will lower your heart rate. Practice when you need it-Practice wherever you can or when you need to. When I worked at a museum as an archaeologist, I used to meditate every day after lunch. I would go out onto our visitors trail on the property and sit on this bench in front of an area that contained wild desert flowers and other various plants. I would focus on something like the flower and breathe deeply and exhale. This always relaxed me, cleared my head and gave me some energy to finish my day. **Stillness**-If you can't practice stillness spontaneously, schedule it throughout your day. **Find a favorite spot. Listen to soft music. Repeat calming phrases**-I am calm and still, etc. over and over to yourself and feel yourself relax. Here is a quote by Hermann Hesse relative to meditation that I would like to share with you. "Within you there is a stillness and a sanctuary to which you can retreat any time." How apropos. It does not get any more succinct than that.

    I would like to briefly mention massage and acupuncture. I personally have never tried either one accept for a massage from my girlfriend once in a while. However, she gets a massage and goes to acupuncture on a regular basis. She says it relieves her stress and relaxes her and helps to release toxins from her body. Every time she comes back from her appointments she is very relaxed. I hate needles so I don't do acupuncture. But, it may be worth your time if you are so inclined.

    There is also one other thing I would like to mention in terms of "natural treatments" for your PTS and trauma in general. One of the very best things you can do is to find an inspiration, or better yet, your passion. What I mean is that there has to be something that you love to do that always makes you feel good when you do it. So, find it and practice it daily. This will also remove you from your problems and put you in a happy spot so to speak where your problems do not exist. For me, there are several things I do. However, the most beneficial one to me is writing. Writing allows me to release pent up emotions in healthy ways thereby rendering those emotionally charged memories to just memories that no longer control my life. I control my life now. Secondly, when I am writing I am so intensely focused on what I am doing that I have no idea what's going on around me five inches from my face. A bomb could go off when I am writing and I wouldn't know it unless it fell in my lap. This is exactly what I am talking about. Your passion will take you away from your trouble and make you happy. You will realize that it does in fact make you feel good so you will begin to do it more and more. Then, before you know it, you are doing it all day long. Next thing you know, you have a whole new life and a brand new career doing what you enjoy and thus, enjoying life.

There are numerous things you can do to achieve this. It is basically whatever makes you happy. You can play guitar, paint, draw, read, sing, run, program a computer, etc. Whatever makes you happy. One of the things that I love to do is cook. So, at night I turn on some jazz music, plan a meal and cook it from scratch. I am completely focused on the task at hand. I relax and escape the world every day by doing this. It brings me great joy and I always feel proud when I create a masterpiece of a meal. Just ask my friends. I quite often send them pictures of the meals I create. Finding your passion is another very important step in the 13 steps I will lay out to you in the last chapter, for you to follow in order to heal your PTS.

Finally, when I was dealing with my PTS I also had very high blood pressure. It was 160 over 106. A healthy blood pressure for someone my age is 140 over 90 with a pulse of 70. So, they treated it just like they were treating my PTS and put me on blood pressure medication right away instead of teaching me to eat healthy things and how to relax in order to lower it naturally. I would also get heart palpitations quite frequently. However, when I started eating better, getting proper nutrition and exercising after I quit all of the psychotropic and blood pressure medications, I was able to drop my blood pressure to very healthy levels. In fact, the last time I took it my blood pressure it was 119 over 85 with a pulse of 59. Better than the recommended level for my age! I dropped it that much just by doing the things I have been talking to you about throughout this chapter. Not only that, I overcame my PTS and got rid of my palpitations. So, obviously your lifestyle and thus proportionately, if not more importantly, your diet can play a huge role in obtaining maximum mental and therefore, physical health. I cannot stress that enough.

"Knowing is not enough; we must apply. Willing is not enough; we must do."

Johann Wolfgang van Goethe
From Dr. Dyer's book, Inspiration: Your Ultimate Calling

MOVE FORWARD

CHAPTER 6

In Jesse Livermore's book, "How to trade in stocks" he references the Marines assaulting a beach. He discusses the analysis which is conducted in order to assault a beach head successfully. He understands that there is no perfect outcome, only the best possible outcome. It is interesting. As a professional archaeologist, I studied groups of Native Americans for 20 years. I could tell you anything you wanted to know about them and all the analytical techniques I used to study such dynamic creatures like humans. You couldn't plug numbers into a mathematical equation and get a specific answer because life is too dynamic, always changing. Just like the stock market.

A lot of archaeologists just couldn't get that through their heads. They were trying to make archaeology an exact science. It was the activities of the group of Indians as a whole that could be ascertained. You could see definite patterns and therefore predict what should happen. I just realized how much the Marines and my career as an archaeologist have prepared me so well for exactly what I am doing now with the stock market and my books. I did these things out of interest yet I didn't know that I was being prepared.

Life and God work in mysterious ways. Life can be very poignant and apropos. Just analyze your life and see what you are being prepared for. My childhood friend Lonnie, was an important part of this book. We had gotten back in touch with each other after 22 years just as I began writing this book. He steered me towards Livermore's book. I told my friend that I wondered what I was supposed to assist him with. This is intriguing.

The Marines taught me to ignore emotion and to do what we were taught, nothing more, nothing less. If you read my first two books, "*A line in the Sand* and *The Chrysalis*," www.robertserocki.com you know about my struggles to accomplish that which I was taught. It wasn't easy. I was up and down. However, in the end and over the long run, I can say I made a profit so to speak. When I was a Marine Sniper I analyzed human patterns based on groups of specific people. After days of analysis, I made a prediction. I then watched to see if it came true and if it did, I struck like a cobra at exactly the right time. I graduated first in my sniper school class. It is one of the toughest schools in all of the entire United States Military.

My experience as an archaeologist was similar. I was ahead of a lot of my peers whom were at the same level as me. I am not trying to brag. I am merely making the point that perhaps I have potential. I always tell myself I will be successful!

In either case, it took time and I couldn't worry about that. I had to focus on the end result I desired and focus on doing something every minute of every day towards accomplishing that no matter how long that took. I always told my men and my staff to always follow the rules. As long as they did that, they wouldn't get into trouble.

While I was writing all of this in my journal, I realized at that exact point I was writing another book. I told my friend to think about when we had met as children. We were inseparable. Then we went 22 years without talking and I had moved to the other side of the country. There we were having this conversation.

I have always told people that I could give them a reason why I met every person in my life. You meet people for a reason. Everything happens for a reason. Keep that in mind and then you will be able to learn from these events of your life which are directly relevant to your own personal success. You must study your own life first before you study anything else in order to learn what you must and hence, become successful with your life. It is a long term commitment. You receive the greatest joy from looking back on your personal journey and seeing just how far you have really come. My, what a ride!

My friend then told me that he had a lot of mistakes to learn from. I told him that we all do. What differentiates one person from another is the person who understands that he or she has made mistakes. Then they realize those mistakes are the Petri dishes that house bacteria whom facilitate learning and thus success. Don't ignore your life lessons. They are truly a gift.

Yes, I have an interest in getting involved in the stock market. Just like I had an interest in joining the Marines and also becoming an archaeologist. These interests I perceive as instincts given to me by God. I do believe that I will be successful in the stock market and make money. However, this is not the actual purpose for me to get involved. I know I will be successful in order to keep my interest in it. There is something that I am supposed to learn from this endeavor just as I did from my experiences in the Marines and in Archaeology. What I do learn needs to be put into a book. That way, it can get to as many people as possible and help as many people as possible. This is my true purpose. This is what I believe

I was put on earth for. To help people heal, become inspired, ***move forward*** and ***be*** successful with their lives after suffering through trauma, such as I did.

At times, things seemed out of control. I was all over the place. I had many irons in the fire. I felt as though I was stretched too thin. How would I ever get everything completed? Well, one must remember that all you need to concern yourself with is to keep going. Move forward every day. Then, at the end of the year, look back on that year and see just how far you have actually come! It is as I said before, it is a long term commitment. Rome was not built in a day. So, whatever is going on remember that all you need to concern yourself with is that you are moving forward every day! That's it.

I hope that with my books (***A Line in the Sand, The Chrysalis and this book*** (www.robertserocki.com) and all of the knowledge, information and experiences I have acquired over the past 25 years or so, will provide you with some insight. I will provide you with an outline to help you to begin your journey to heal and become successful. This outline is not a set in stone guideline. I wrote it as a guide for anyone to follow. But remember, this is YOUR journey. It is directly relative to you and your own personal experiences. However, you must have a plan to begin. Always remember that plans change and often they change thousands of times. So, if you don't have a plan to begin with, you will be completely lost and fail. The biggest reason new businesses fail, especially in their first year, is because of poor planning or no plan at all. You need something in the beginning from which to work from In order to get your start. It is up to you to study, make the right decisions on the basis of your analysis, and move forward. No one can do that for you. Nor will they.

So, I am providing you with a starting point. ***You*** must take it from there. My intent is to help you ***move forward*** without having to suffer from as many of the setbacks I had to endure because at the time I began my journey I did not have the knowledge I am providing you with now. It is like Jesse Livermore says in his book, "How to trade in stocks," "Develop your own strategy, discipline and approach to the market. I offer my suggestions as one who has traveled the road before you. Perhaps I can act as a guide for you and save you from falling into some of the pitfalls that befell me. But, in the end the decisions must be your own."

Through my journey I found that when I was on a downward spiral I spent most of my time trying to figure out how to get out of doing things or making appointments. Let this be a warning to you that you are moving in the wrong direction. You should be spending most of your time on trying to figure out how to get more things accomplished and enacting your plan, not how to get out of them. This reminds me of one of my favorite quotes.

"Yes, you have been through all this before, replies his heart. But you have never been beyond it. Then the Warrior realizes that these repeated experiences have but one aim: to teach him what he does not want to learn." Paulo Coelho*: Warrior of the Light, a Manual* 2003.

I recently spent a week in bed because of my lower back. I have problems with it since I got out of my wheelchair. I also had been working 17 hour days for quite some time and was feeling quite horrible. At first, I got upset that everything seemed to be falling apart again. However, I quickly focused and realized that my feeling bad and my back hurting was a sign. A sign that I needed to slow down and re-focus on my mission and what is really important. So, I decided to enjoy myself and once I was able to get up and walk around I went for a hike in the desert. While I was there, I became inspired almost immediately and words started flowing to me. All I had was my cell phone. So, I started texting my very good friend Lonnie. I was texting him again with the words that were being given to me. I was on another roll.

Yes my back still hurts from time to time, but sometimes when life pushes you have to push back. Life is about choices. You pay a price for any choice you make, good or bad. So make the choices that make you happy and don't be afraid to pay the price for your decision. I have made mine. My life is what it is because of the choices I made and continue to make. I have found my purpose in life. I know why I am here. I live my life to accomplish that mission. My back hurting and I feeling horrible for a week was a warning from my body. It was telling me to slow down and refocus. I was losing sight of what was most important to me.

As long as you are fulfilling your true purpose, you will be provided for. It's not something I read. It's something I have lived. When I was at my lowest, crippled, compromised by Post Traumatic Stress, no food, no shelter, I was provided with Frida. She then provided me with the things I needed. Not because I am great, but because I am focused. I have an awareness. So, make those necessary choices. Figure out what your purpose is and do it. The rest will simply be amazing.

I was sitting on top of a mountain at 2200 feet, texting these messages to Lonnie. I was there with a great view, some water, a granola bar and myself. It was awesome. The world is an amazing place. I love the desert. I am truly a desert rat. I have lived in it, fought in it, lived off of it and enjoyed its beauty. I have seen things born and die in it.

I remember backpacking in the mountains of the Arizona desert with Frida before I ended up in my wheelchair. We would spend the entire weekend out there living off of the land. We ate flowers, cactus fruit, seeds, jojoba beans and some trout I stabbed with my knife in a stream. We purified the water. I even know how to make my own water.

I taught Frida how to survive. How to depend on no one except herself and God. The Marines taught me how to survive no matter what and I try to pass that on to others. Enjoy your freedom and your freedom to choose to do whatever you want as long as it is within the boundaries of the law. You have been given a great gift. Don't be foolish and waste it.

I sit in the desert and I watch lizards dart back and forth quickly because their feet are burning like bacon in a hot frying pan. I watch Gamble quail strut around like chickens and watch their top knots bounce like a ponytail in someone's hair as they run. I listen to the sharp, pierce, yet beautiful chirp of the Cactus Wren as it echoes through the desert canyon. I see the beautiful flowers and breathtaking views. I watch things die and things get born.

I reflect on the fact that right in front of my face is a message. Physical things come and go. However, life itself continues in perpetuity. There is beauty in that. Life is profound if we just pay attention. I can say, for a moment at least, I am truly at peace.

You see, life is more than hope. Hope, is false. If you only "hope" for things, then you are putting your faith in something that does not exist yet. Believe in YOURSELF! If you want it, you can have it. Do what you have to do to get it. If you don't take action, hope won't do anything for you accept let you down. Just like the famous stock market investor Jessie Livermore said when he talked about investors who HOPE their stocks do well and how they always failed. Put your money on yourself and God. That's all anyone needs. It really is that simple.

All things that happen in our lives happen for a reason. In my book, "*Chrysalis*" I discuss and analyze all the dreams I had for many years. Those dreams had a common theme to them, which was difficulty. They were foretelling all the difficulties I would face in my life if I did not face my problems. These difficulties would repeat themselves until I actually moved past my problems.

As luck would have it, I met a colleague in my career as an archaeologist. He brought my attention to the great Psychoanalyst, Carl Jung. Jung analyzed the works of Sigmund Freud. From Jung's books, I learned how to interpret my dreams and learn from them. Many people dismiss their dreams as erratic absurdity. However, they are not. They are personalized messages sent directly to you for your own edification. They are erratic and outlandish, some might say, in order for you to remember them just like a Native American mythology. Carl Jung said, "Dreaming has meaning, like everything else we do. No psychic (or physical) fact is accidental. The events which do not awaken any strong emotions have little influence on our thoughts or actions, whereas those which provoke strong emotional reactions are of great importance for our subsequent psychological development."

My Grandfather, on my mother's side of the family, was a big influence on my life. I know that he was in my life for a reason. He taught me about reading, education, and books. Because of that I went to college and got a degree in Anthropology, with an emphasis on Archaeology. With that, I got a job as an archaeologist and met my boss, whom over the course of the next 16 years, honed my analytical skills and taught me how to write.

Then, I suffered many trials and tribulations associated with Post Traumatic Stress. That ultimately gave me the material I needed in order to write my books, which I now do full time.

No one's life is insignificant. There are reasons you are here and there are reasons you go through what you go through. Learn your lessons wisely and apply them to your life. The world, the galaxy and the cosmos are infinite. So, why would you think that yourself (i.e. the life within you) is not one in the same? The minerals and properties found within your teeth, bones, muscles and blood are all also things that comprise the earth.

We all need to understand that our "work" is the work of a lifetime. We need to focus on "moving forward" each and every day. No matter how small or insignificant this progress may seem it is progress and thus, moving forward. Those are the things we need to focus on, the positive things. If you always focus on the bad things, or negativity, then that's what you will bring into your life until you end the whole negative cycle.

Life is analogous to the stock market. There are many ups and downs throughout the day, week, months and year. But, what you look at is the positive growth you have achieved over a long term period. This concept is reflected in the basic economic principle that you want a profit on investment, it is more long term and more lucrative versus profit on individual sales. That is short term, cyclical and very erratic.

This is how I view, analyze and learn from my own life. I don't worry so much about the day to day operations or events of it. Yes, I pay attention to things, but my focus is to move forward every day. For instance, every year at the end of the year, I take time to reflect on my life over the past year and previous years. From that, I make a plan for the following year. Then, I implement it and apply what I have learned to my philosophy of always moving forward.

This way I can see the accomplishment and achievements I have made because they are much bigger and more significant over a year's time versus day to day. So, I know that by moving forward each day I am making progress. I don't focus on exactly what or how much I have actually accomplished until the end of the year. This way it has a much bigger impact on me. I remember it more clearly and because of the impact it has on me, it helps me to stay focused.

Donald Trump and Bill Zanker wrote a book called, "Think Big and Kick Ass!" A paragraph in that book struck me profoundly, "The biggest doers in life often suffer the biggest setbacks in life. So, if you want to aim high, you have to have the guts to handle the inevitable bumps in the road!"

In other words, the bigger the things you do, the bigger risks there are. Without risk, there is no gain. The bigger the risk, the higher the gain! Remember, every action has a direct and proportionate reaction.

When I was younger and I would complain about things, my father would always ask me, "Of all the successful people you know, how old do you think they are?" I would reply, "Old I guess. In their 60's. Why do you think that is son? Why do you think you did not meet them until then? I don't know Dad." He then replied, "Because they spent all those years busting their butts instead of complaining like you!" When he told me this I would get angry and stomp away. I now clearly understand the wisdom behind his saying. It has definitely had a big impact on my life.

I remember sitting in my condo that I used to own many years ago and having a conversation with God. He told me I would lose everything, but it would be ok. Eventually, I did lose everything, just like God had said. I now know why. The slate had to be cleaned in order for me to accomplish my most important of goals, which was to be a writer. I was angry and upset when it happened. But now I understand that life is much, much bigger than just you and I. There are much greater forces at work here than human beings just living their lives on one planet in a galaxy of others in an infinite cosmos. It's all taken care of. We just have to pay attention to our messages.

Humans get upset at things and break down. Then, they punish themselves with alcohol and drugs, which create a false, short lived euphoria that only comes back to bite you two fold later. The more you do it, the worse it becomes. Why do we put our faith in such things? Drugs and alcohol only place a barrier between you and your divinity. It's like a wall around a castle. Nothing can get in or out. So, if your punishing yourself with these things (because that's what you are really doing) stop it.

If you keep doing this then you perpetually become permanently separated. Once that occurs, the physical self-starts a pre-mature decay. This can be halted, if one reconnects. I like to use the analogy of a rechargeable battery. If you do not plug it in, it loses its charge. You can recharge it by plugging it back in. However, if you keep it unplugged too long, the rechargeable celldies and it will no longer hold a charge and you must discard it. This I believe, is what happens to the physical self if you keep it unplugged from its source of energy.

To exemplify what I am saying, I recently had a friend who passed away much too young. He served in the Army during Viet Nam. He carried a lot of pain around within him. He dealt with it by drinking and doing drugs. I understood the pain and suffering as I too served my county during war as a Marine. I have also suffered through punishing myself with things that create a false sense of reality. However, I stopped and plugged myself back into my source and he did not. He paid the ultimate price for it. I am not saying that my physical body will never die. I am simply saying that he passed much too pre-maturely before he got to impact mankind with the purpose he was put on earth for because he ignored his source. He never got to feel the joy of fulfilling his primary purpose for a physical existence. This, is very sad.

I do however, understand that in society today money makes the world go round. I understand that we must go out into the world to do things in order to make money to survive. I also understand that this is the system in which we live. So, I learn it and understand it so that I may accomplish my purpose within it. It is sort of like Benjamin Franklin used to say, "Industry and frugality are the means of procuring wealth and thereby securing virtue." He also used to say that, "You cannot judge a man's wealth by what he has in his wallet. You judge it by what he has given to mankind." Most of the books he read were controversial or contentious works that dealt with God like, deific or trans mundane occurrences and or, people. This is something to definitely contemplate. Especially since he was so successful. In fact, if my memory serves me correctly, he was the only person to sign all three documents that formed the United States of America. They are the Constitution, the Declaration of Independence, and the Peace Treaty with France. Pretty good credentials, don't you think?

I was looking at a house plant a moment ago that my girlfriend brought home from work and placed on our breakfast bar. It was going to be thrown away because it was dying. I check the soil to see if it is dry and if it is, I water it. I open the blinds so that it gets sunlight during the day. Now the plant is bright green and flourishing.

I also consider the fact that the other night when I said my prayers, I asked God about the subject of self-improvement. I had a dream that night that I was inside a large, rather old tree. I was pruning all of the dead branches off of it one at a time. It was hard work and very time consuming. Every time I cut away a dead branch, the tree flourished a little bit more. It was a continuous process of infinite improvement as long as I stayed focused on what needed to be done.

I contemplate these two aforementioned things and I cannot help but pontificate on the fact that this is how life is and I have just been presented with two divine messages affirming my aforementioned hypotheses that as long as we do what we were put here on Earth to do, everything will fall into place and be taken care of for us.

Recently I became frustrated. After seven years of working to overcome PTS, instead of just existing with it, I am tired and frustrated. All of the traumatic experiences and battles have taken their toll on me. I need a break. Here I now find myself with $14 in my savings account, $4 in my pocket and $0 in my checking account. I feel let down to have come all this way and end up not even being able to pay a bill. I was falling into a bad mental state. So, I laced up my hiking boots and headed to the mountain. It is a place I have been visiting since I was a teenager. I also worked there as an archaeologist. I visit there now to rest my mind, reconnect with my spirit and energize my sole.

After 20 minutes of being in this special place, I realized just how far I have come and how much I have accomplished. I am out of my wheelchair, lost 60 pounds, got off of all of my medication, have a place to live, beat the PTS and I am now playing the stock market and writing books. I speak to people on how to deal with grief and heal. A lot people don't ever make it out of the hospital or off of their meds, let alone being productive again. I must refocus now and realize I have come a long way but still have a ways to go. I am good and I am doing a good job. I thanked the Mountain for providing this spot to focus and for re-energizing my sole and helping me to see what's really important. Now I can move forward again and continue with my journey.

I must absolutely trust that I will be given what I need. I have to. It is as my very good friend Lonnie recently told me. He said that him and I just can't live normal lives. We simply cannot get a job, buy a mutual fund and retire. I must be true to that. I know I have a purpose here as I think we all do. I understand mine and I am willing to take that journey and face whatever I encounter. I am willing to pay the price for my choices whether they are good or bad results. Are you? Do you have that courage to make the decision and have even more courage to enact it? This you must find in order to move forward and eventually, truly become happy. I have found it. You can too. I am back on the straight and narrow path. Thank God for this mountain.

Realistically speaking, life is like the stock market. You must cut your losses. If you don't, you will always be in the hole even when you do make a gain. Same in life. You must cut out the bad. If not, it's like climbing up a rung on a ladder and then getting knocked back two rungs. Then, you have to climb back up three rungs in order to get ahead again. In other words, you are always in a deficit and always trending towards the down side. You must have the discipline to develop good habits and keep them. You always have to analyze them and adapt them as you go on your journey. It's a constant, dynamic process of change and improvement.

So, here I am again. It is 4:30am and I am sitting on my patio in June. I awoke at 4am today with a voice in my head telling me to get up and write. So, I got up and I am going to do just that. I have done this many times before. Especially when I was writing my second book, the Chrysalis. It seems that this is the best time for me to write. It is peaceful now. There are no distractions and my ideas flow to me as easily as an ocean wave rolls upon the shore.

Everyone is asleep. Well, almost everyone. There are a few brave souls, such as me, who are awake to challenge the old standard of nine to five and seize the day. Or, perhaps more apropos, "The early bird gets the worm." How about, "Early to bed, early to rise. Makes a man healthy, wealthy and wise." I think that one is my favorite as I can't help but take some solace and glean some hope from its somewhat esoteric meaning.

I truly enjoy being up at this hour in the morning writing. It is as if I escape to another world or perhaps some other dimension in time. It is like my primary senses switch to secondary ones. Almost like going from Earth into outer space and switching from gravity to weightlessness. My soul is alive and it feels energized as creativity and ideas bounce around in my head like popcorn in a corn popper.

Writing has to be one of the greatest things I have ever done other than following my heart, my passion, or as I lovingly call it, my divine inspiration. As long as I follow it, things always seem to work out for me. Perhaps at the moment things are happening to me that may seem bleak, but looking back on things sometime later always reveals that my course in life has been guided by a gentle, but firm hand.

I have experienced what some people call the full circle of life. I have brought life into this world. I have taken it out. I have even died once myself, when my heart stopped beating for a minute in a restaurant when I was in my twenties and I took a little trip to a bright white light before I awoke. However, I am still amazed at the cycle of things. All of its beginnings and endings. All of its birth and death. To me life never seems to die. That energy is infinite. It's right there in front of your face. Just look out your window and try to deny its commanding existence.

It seems at times, and more often for some than others, naivety creeps into our lives and takes hold of us like a bad cancer using the cells in your body as a host and ultimately destroying them. Why do we let this word, this actual lack of pure, analytical, autarchic thought invade our minds and thus our lives? Do you really want to believe that life really is so mundane? That life is so matter of fact that we are all born, we live unfulfilled lives of labor only to die and become food for worms?

There is no logical way anyone could possibly believe that to be true about life. Just take a look at yourself. Do you really understand the dynamic processes that occur within your body every day? Take an unbiased look at the world around you. Can you still look me in the face and tell me all of our lives are un-purposeful?

If you answered yes to that question, then perhaps your life is in fact unpurposeful. But, understand that if it is, then it is only because you have made it that way. It is no one else's fault but your own. You may put blame, or even heap abuse on others. Ultimately, your life has always been up to you. You have chosen to be blind even though you may physically be able to see. You have chosen to be ignorant even though you have the ability to think and learn. Why would you give up the one and only thing that makes you human?

I have wrestled with this "What makes us human question" since my college days, when it was proposed to me by my Anthropology professor. Only then, I did not know that it would become my life long profession to answer it and teach the world what I have learned.

The sun is rising now. Its pure golden light is shining on the tree tops in front of my patio. It reminds me of when I was in the Saudi Arabian desert, during the first Gulf War, and the sun would rise in the morning providing me with its glow. It signified the ending of the danger of the night and the fact that I was one day closer to going home. Imagine what my life would be like now, if back then when I was told 90% of us would die the first day, I succumbed myself to the naïve thought that life is merely a monochromatic endeavor? Somehow, someway, no matter how bad it got, I found a way to continue. I was holding on to the fact that I knew my life, as does everyone else's, had a purpose and that purpose would be fulfilled unless I chose to ignore it.

Every day, I struggle with trying to get everything done all at once. I have to constantly remind myself that things take time. Rome was not built in a day. This is my life's work. It will take a lifetime to accomplish. So, don't be in a hurry to get it over with. Just hang on and enjoy the ride. Enjoy as much of it as you possibly can.

I have been taught about patience my whole life. As a kid I had to be patient in December waiting for Christmas to come. I had to be patient during the school year waiting for summer vacation to come so I could go visit my dad and friends in Michigan. I had to be patient at night in my bed in boot camp waiting for graduation day to come. I had to be patient in sniper school waiting for just the right time to take the perfect shot. I had to be patient waiting to hear back from the interview board to see if I got my first job as a professional archaeologist and I have to be patient wondering if I will ever get to see or talk to my son again.

You see, there is a lesson here. While we must be patient, we must also understand that there are things that are just out of our control. Things do and will take time, but we simply cannot sit around idle doing nothing. You have to keep moving forward and pursuing your inner desires. As long as you are doing that then you will achieve the much bigger goals you are striving for. If you do just one thing and sit around waiting for your big dream to happen, it won't. The monotony would drive you nuts and it should precipitate you to keep going forward in order to accomplish your dreams. Good things come to those who wait, but even better and bigger things come to those who keep doing while knowing that their desires will be fulfilled as long as they keep moving down their path.

For instance, I had to work very hard through three months of pure hell to achieve my goal of being a Marine. I had to muster the energy every day to go to college full time, work two jobs, do volunteer work on the weekend for nearly six years in order to fulfill my dreams of being an archaeologist. I had to spend many months to learn how to invest my money, spending long hours doing research late into the night in order to be a stock market investor properly. I spent many, many hours reading and learning and applying what I learned in order to overcome PTS. I wrote hundreds of pages at four in the morning when it was peaceful most days of the week before I had to go exercise two hours and then work a full day in order to fulfill my dreams of being an author and getting my books published.

All of these things took a very long time to accomplish and I suffered through many trials and tribulations along the way. I even got knocked off of my path several times thinking my dreams were being squashed. But, I always found a way to get back up off of the ground and keep moving forward.

All of these things that I have accomplished were all goals of mine. They all put a fire in my belly. I kept moving from one goal to the next, not even understanding what I was really doing, what I was really being "molded" for. There is a much, much bigger purpose for all of this. Each one of these goals are a piece of a bigger puzzle, they are pieces to the foundation of a building. They are rungs in a ladder to take me from the ground to the sky.

My father and the Marines made me strong, gave me discipline, taught me work ethic and responsibility in order to be able to persevere and accomplish things in life no matter how bad my situation is. They helped me muster the strength and courage to finish college while working two jobs and suffering from the ill effects of PTS. College taught me how to read, study and learn. It gave me the foundation of knowledge I needed to become an archaeologist. The two jobs and volunteer work gave me some preliminary skills and allowed me to network so one day I could get a job with the City working for the City Archaeologist. My job as the assistant archaeologist to the City archaeologist gave me the opportunity to meet this man who over the course of the next 16 years, honed my analytical and research skills and taught me how to write. With those skills I became an author and in some time, an investor.

So, you can clearly see that all of these "pieces" of my life fit together quite well. What I had to realize is that I was going somewhere. All of these accomplished goals have taken me to the doorstep of the next much bigger, stage of my life. I did not plan it this way. I just followed my dreams and they led me here. I now know that I will become wealthy and not just in money. My books and my endeavors in the stock market will bring me there and that will enhance my life tremendously after everything I have been through. I also know that when I achieve this new found wealth, it won't just be for the sole purpose of making me happy. It's like a carrot being dangled in front of my nose while I am hungry in order to keep me moving forward. Because once I get to that point, I will need to use my new life as an example to others that they too can heal and become successful with their lives just like me. I am not unique in this cycle of things. You can, and are meant to be part of it as well, as long as you pay attention. Once I do teach the world what I know, I can only imagine where it will lead me next!

It is never too late to set things straight. I have heard a lot of people say, "I am too old now. I have been doing this for too long for me to change now and start over." Or, they simply say, "I don't have the time." You can always do something towards achieving your goals or pursuing your passion. You also have all the time in the world. There are 24 hours in every day. I know we must sleep and you may even have a full time job, or even young kids to raise. However, if you actually get eight hours of sleep a night and work full time, you still have eight additional hours every day to play with and more on the weekends! Say you are raising young children and they take all the rest of that time. Fine, those children are part of your purpose in life. You were meant to bring those children into this world and/or raise them even if they are someone else's kids. Some people just can't have kids. Eventually, they do grow up and become self-sufficient. At the very most, that will take 18 years. Then, you get all of that time back in order to pursue your next goal.

I can hear all of the excuses coming at this very moment. I know because I have done it as well. But, once I stopped wasting time making excuses and I started doing, my life changed significantly the very moment I did so. While yes, I may not know the particular circumstances of your very individual lives, but I do know a lot about life and how to live it.

Me writing all of this and you reading it is very analogous to people who grow up, raise kids and teach them what they know in order to help them find their way in the world. I know that technically all of you are not my children, but I am living my life and teaching you what I know just the same. It's like my dad always said when I asked his advice on something, "Don't make the same mistakes I did. It's already been done!"

The days are getting quite long now. It is coming upon the longest day of the year, June 21st. The official start of summer. A whole new cycle will begin and ultimately end. Just like every cycle of your life. Even if it is a bad cycle, it will end. Trust me, it will. I know this because that is just life. Every day marks the beginning of something new and the ending of something old. So, make the best of it!

Regular life has a way of getting in the way of our goal driven lives. For instance my girlfriend just got up and was getting ready to walk the dog. She told me she wants to apply for a part time job in order to pay off some of her bills and be able to at least have a down payment for a new car. She already has a full time job for which she is gone from seven in the morning until six at night five days a week. My first reaction was to think about who is going to walk the dog then when I am gone on a business trip? I will have to be the one who has to clean the house, do the grocery shopping, and cook all the meals myself after working 14 hours a day and exercising two hours a day, sometimes seven days a week. Normally, we split all of the chores 50/50. Then I thought great, this is all going to keep me from accomplishing my goals now.

But, I realize I can't think that. That is such a narrow minded way to look at things. I am human and I do screw up sometimes just like everyone else. I have to realize that she also has her own life, her own path, her own goals and she must be allowed to go and accomplish those things just as I must be allowed to do the same thing. It will all work out. It always does. She will find a way to do her thing, I will find a way to do mine and we will find a way to do "our" things together.

I am not any different than any of you. Things happen to me just like they do to you. The only difference may be that when things do happen to me, I have developed the ability to catch myself before I fall so to speak. I used to fall before and sometimes stay down for a while, before I actually realized what was going on and got back up. I have made that adjustment. It took time and practice to develop it and apply it properly.

Sometimes the body gets tired when one is trying to do so much. Sleep is a beautiful thing and so is coffee. There was a time in my life when I couldn't sleep. Not even for an hour. Sometimes I would go for weeks with only sleeping an hour a night if I was lucky. It was because my PTS had gotten so bad that it even took away my body's natural, inherent ability to rest and recharge. I didn't know what was wrong with me. I just figured eventually I would get so exhausted that I would collapse and sleep. But, that never happened. So, I ignored it and eventually it caught up with me as to say, "Hey, I am still here. You can't ignore me!" Ultimately, I broke down completely.

It was in the hospital where my new adventure had begun. They put me on even more medication and increased my therapy. Once I got out of the hospital, I continued seeing my regular doctor and I moved forward with my healing process. I did well for a while, but this whole cycle repeated itself once again. I went through all of this for six years before I got better, before I actually felt complete again. I thought to myself as I was going through all of this that I did not want all of this to have been done in vain. I was trying to figure out what I would do with my new life once I got better. So, I wrote my second book about it, *The Chrysalis* (www.robertserocki.com). It was while I was writing this book that I discovered the new direction I would take down my path of life.

I remember all of the pain, fear, dysentery and hunger I suffered through and all of the blood, sweat and tears that were shed when I was in the war. I kept that all bottled up and hidden like preserves vacuum sealed in a mason jar for twelve years before I decided to let it out and face it. So, as I did with the last phase of my life, I wrote my first book about it, *A Line in the Sand*.

Sometimes I think that I should have faced it all sooner and saved myself a lot of time and extra suffering. But, if I had not allowed myself to go through all of that no matter how long it took, I would not have been able to write the two books I previously mentioned and I wouldn't have acquired all of the knowledge you are reading about in this, my third book, that I have written.

Things do happen for a reason. I am a firm believer in that. Nothing is wasted in your life unless you yourself choose to ignore it. Yes, while you are going through these events of your life, you may not understand the purpose behind it all until you have been through it, until you have completed the cycle and look back upon it and reflect. That's why I love New Year's Eve. Most people think it's just a holiday set aside for people to get drunk and relish in debauchery. It is not. It is a holiday set aside in order to help you to schedule the time to reflect upon the past years events and based upon that, plan your goals for the following year. I take full advantage of every New Year's Eve. I do not waste that time every year with idolatry, debauchery and wickedness. I use that opportunity I have been given to reflect, move forward and plan to be better the following year.

It's five in the morning and the sun is starting it's ascent into our eastern horizon. The doves are cooing and the other birds have begun their songs. They are all flying back and forth now as if they all are jockeying for position in the morning chow hall line. The moon is directly above me right now, but only half full. It is half way through its descent to another part of the world that will be going to bed soon.

It is Tuesday today and I begin my week with some trepidation and excitement. I just received my shipment of my new book, **The Chrysalis**, yesterday and this week I am putting some of my books in a book store, doing a book signing, a radio show and a live TV show about my life and my books.

I had to prepare some questions to give to the TV station producer for the show hosts to ask me that would be informative for their viewers and give them something to work from. So, I came up with six of them. Most of the questions are pretty basic. Who am I? What's my background? Etc. The last few questions are as follows: Why did you write these books? What is the message of your books? How do your books relate to what is going on in the world now with Iraq and the Veteran's Administration scandals?

The reason I wrote the books is quite simple. My first book, *A Line in the Sand*, was a cathartic process for me. It was the beginning to my healing journey that I was unknowingly embarking upon. It was a way for me to get the "war" off of my chest and tell my story. People would ask me about the war and I didn't like talking about it back then. So, this way I could simply hand them a book. I wrote the second book, *Chrysalis*, as I was going through my healing process. I remembered how much writing the first book helped me unload that baggage so I knew it would help me again. I remember sitting in my doctor's office back then before I began writing the book and I told her I was done writing. I had nothing more to write about and that no one cared anyways. She said, "I beg to differ. I think you have a lot to write about." Well, here we are three books later.

The message of my books is this: Veterans need to tell their stories not only for the catharsis it will bring to them, but to educate the world. Also, every life on this planet has a purpose to fulfill. No life is insignificant. You just have to be willing to pay attention and follow your inspiration. Everyone can heal, become inspired, move forward and be successful with their lives!

Just this past weekend, yet again, there was some more turmoil in my life. My girlfriend had been having some difficulties in her life. She was having trouble remembering things, even things I had just spoken to her an hour ago. Her speech was abrupt and fragmented. She didn't care about anything and ignored everything. This led to the point where she wasn't paying the bills. I had been lecturing her about the importance of this for many months. However, nothing changed and it got to the point where our electricity was shut off and in the same day I got a notice in the mail that our automobile insurance was cancelled. I became furious. I had told her not to let this happen and yet she did. I had been trying to help her and teach her, but she just couldn't make the effort. So, I decided I had to put my foot down. I gave her an ultimatum. She had 24 hours to decide whether she was going to stay here living with me, or she would move out and be on her own. I simply couldn't take it anymore.

She decided she was going to leave. After another day of thinking about this, I came up with another idea so she could stay and I could try and help her again. I owe her that much. I needed to relieve the stress in her life for her so she could think clearly. It was obviously affecting her. I knew that because of how she was acting. I went through the same thing when I was dealing with my PTS. I couldn't think, speak or even remember anything from one hour to the next. She liked my idea and decided to stay. She immediately started doing better. I gave her the idea that she needed to find a hobby, something fun in her life to do outside of work. So, a few days later she found something she wanted to do involving art.

A few days later, I was sitting in my office working. I looked over by my TV stand and saw a copy of my second book, **Chrysalis**, sitting there. I picked it up and thumbed through it and ended up on page 29 where I wrote about a dream I had on January 7, 2004. The dream discussed a women that I was going to meet that would be in my life forever and how our relationship would have difficulties and we would have to change direction. Well, here we are. I have been with her more than a decade. We have had our difficulties. We had to very recently change direction just like the dream I had 10 years ago told me, which was eight months before I ever met her.

Now, she is doing better and so are we. She started applying for different jobs and over the course of a few months and numerous interviews she got a new job which was a promotion for her. I kept telling her not to give up. Keep trying and keep networking. Eventually it will pay off and it did. Now, if something happens to me and I lose all of my money and/or can't work we will still be comfortable and able to live because of her raise.

Life has its ups and downs even as you go through the healing process. You must let the bad things roll off of your shoulders, focus on the good and MOVE FORWARD no matter what happens.

Eventually you will get to where you need to go. Remember, the healing process is continuous and dynamic. It is completely normal to have your good days and bad. It is also normal to have relapses along the way. So try not to get discouraged and focus on the task at hand.

I would like to leave you with something to contemplate while you consider what I have written so far and also to help you begin your journey towards healing as you read the next very important chapter. It is a quote from Epictetus whom was a Greek philosopher. "It is difficulties that show what men are." Here is one more relevant quote, which I believe also requires some contemplation as you take your journey. This quote is from a book called, "John Adams" by David McCullough. This was something that Mr. Adams would tell his son John Quincy when he became discouraged, "Patience and perseverance will carry you with honor through all difficulties."

"The best way to learn is through studying the history of successes and failures in your industry."

Donald Trump from his book Think Big and Kick Ass In Business and Life, 2007.

YOUR FOUNDATION TO HEALING

CHAPTER 7

In the sections of this chapter that follow, I describe each step in my 13 step foundation which can guide you as you embark on your journey to heal. Each section and thus each step, is in chronological order. They are intended to be read and followed in that manner as each step builds upon each other and then leads to the next. By studying these steps in such a manner you will obtain an understanding on how to build a strong foundation for yourself that will facilitate you achieving a successful, happy life. The foundation is important. Take a house for example. If you try to build a house without a foundation, it will crumble. However, if you build a solid foundation first, that house can withstand just about anything. Even if the house falls, you still have a foundation to begin building upon once again and this is very important. Once you have a solid foundation, no matter what happens to you, you will be able to recover. Once you build this foundation, you will be ready to go out into the world again and achieve any dream you want. It is at this point that the world itself becomes your oyster. Some of the sections that follow are long and others are short. At the end of these sections, I provide an outline of these 13 steps for you. This book contains all the information, resources and details you need to begin to embark on your journey and build your foundation. It is a convenient, handy resource that is readily accessible to you just like a bible. So, keep it with you so that you can reference it any time you need.

1). ACCEPTANCE

The very first step to take in your journey is acceptance. You must accept responsibility for your life and the decisions you made because you own them. No one else does. You are going through what you are going through, feeling what you're feeling and in the position you are in, because of the decisions that you have made. Every decision you have made put you in the position to receive whatever has happened to you, good or bad. You must realize this and accept it or you will not be able to move forward from here.

Basically, what you are doing is making yourself understand the fact that you make decisions regarding your life and its outcome on a daily basis. You then begin to realize that if you do not like the results you are getting (i.e., the outcome of your life thus far) then you need to make new/different decisions to get your desired outcome. You are the one that must do this. No one else can do this for you because it's your life not theirs. In other words you are the one in control, no one else. Same thing with your PTS as with your life. Accept responsibility for making the decision that put you in a position to get PTS and accept the fact that you still have it because you haven't yet made the decision to heal from it. I hear people say all the time that you can't get rid of PTS, it never goes away. This is simply not true at all. I know. I had PTS for more than 20 years and overcame it with the methods I am outlining in this chapter.

If you enjoy having PTS, then there is no need to read any further as you must already be happy. If you don't enjoy having PTS, then accept responsibility for it and your life and make the decision to get better. You can be happy and at peace once again. I realize this all may seem a bit harsh, but it's the truth. Once you accept responsibility you will realize you are in control and once you understand that, you will have the confidence and determination you need to embark upon this journey and heal properly. This in the end will make you even stronger!

Acceptance is the realization that to err is divine. It is knowing that inspirations and ideas are given to you freely. Your choices effect events in your life for the purpose of teaching you that which you do not know, that which you do not want to learn, and to cause you to take the proper path to your destiny. This astute understanding and allowing underscores the complexity to which all things in your life are organized to perfection. You then see no other choice but to accept your life and all its events in their totality with the understanding that it is divine intervention and that you yourself, as are all people, cupped in the hands of God.

Acceptance is homologous to leaping off a cliff blindfolded while having the cognition to see that you are never really in any danger. It is trusting that your life is laid out in front of you like a road and you contain the ability to read it like a map. You must allow yourself to perceive the spiritual intervention in your life with the ultimate trust that this must be and you must make it so.

ACCEPTANCE
Acknowledging
Certain
Choices
Effect

Personal
Tasks
And
Noting
Changes
Experienced

ACCEPTANCE

2). AWARENESS

One thing you need to realize about the healing process is to make sure you "take time to heal." Most people do not give themselves enough time to heal properly or complete the process. It is a long term commitment and the amount of time it takes for a person to heal is different for each individual. So, you must be patient and commit yourself in the beginning to heal no matter how long that takes for you. It is something you must accept before you begin your journey.

When I started my journey, I asked my civilian doctor how long this would take as I wanted to finish the process as quick as possible because I wanted to feel good again. She told me that the length of time was different for everyone and dependent upon the individual. She also said it could take a year, two years, three years or more. She just did not know and had no way of knowing. That sort of let the air out of my tires at the time, but now I understand the wisdom behind her answer.

It simply is just going to take time. Give yourself that. You deserve it. Don't be too hard on yourself and don't punish yourself for not "getting healed" in a short amount of time. It is like the doctor also told me, "You have spent 20 years suffering from this. It is going to take time to heal from that and all the damage it has caused." That put things in perspective for me rather quickly. I got it.

Your trauma is really a blessing in disguise. You can learn from it and grow from it and you can most certainly become a better person for it. So, use your gift wisely and do not waste it. Thereby turning what was once considered a negative experience into a positive one.

When my PTS really started bothering me it was manifesting itself in ways that I did not understand. I did not know why I was having certain problems. At times, I didn't even know I was having issues and that they were affecting my everyday life. Sometimes, I just couldn't see it. I just couldn't make that connection.

The PTS was causing me to stutter, have choppy speech, unclear and incomplete thought patterns. I could not remember facts, things I read and hour before hand, or things people told me. The nerves in my eye lid would twitch uncontrollably. I simply couldn't concentrate on anything. These are things to look out for. If you are exhibiting these traits, it may be time to take inventory of your life and assess your situation. When you don't deal with trauma it will manifest itself in all types of ways, such as the ones I mentioned above. The more you suppress or ignore these things and your trauma, the worse it will become over time. You have to be completely honest with yourself and admit that you are having trouble.

These "symptoms" of unresolved trauma that I have just mentioned manifest themselves in a lot of people no matter your race, gender or status in life. I have friends who in the past, have exhibited these same symptoms to me and I knew something was wrong. I knew it because I had been through it all before. However, when I asked them what was wrong they would always tell me, "nothing." Even when I mentioned that I had been through this before and I exhibited those same symptoms, they still would not acknowledge something was wrong. This "ignoring" of the self and its issues will only cause greater turmoil. So, if you are exhibiting these symptoms, take stock of what is going on and identify what is bothering you. It is your body's way of telling you, "Hello, something is wrong!"

So, your very second step in the recovery process is to develop an awareness of self and what is going on with you. You have to understand what is going on with you and why. I will give you a few examples. We can use my story about how the color orange used to bother me as the first example.

Every morning and every evening when the sun rose or set, it would cast an orange glow over the landscape. I would start to get nervous, my heart rate would rise, my heart beat harder, my alertness levels would rise dramatically. I never knew why at certain times of the day this would happen.

So, I decided that this was something I was going to pay attention too. Every time that this happened from that moment on I was going to "take stock" of everything in my environment. I was going to analyze the situation and learn from it.

One morning when I woke up a little after sunrise, I opened my blinds to let the light in and I walked over to my dresser to get my clothes for the day. I began to panic again. I quickly remembered that I was going to focus on what was going on around me.

I recalled everything I did from the time I woke until that moment and how I felt. I remembered that when I awoke I felt fine but that right then I was at a heightened sense of alert. "When did this happen?" I realized it happened after I opened the blinds on my window. I then asked myself, "What changed in my environment when I did that?"

I suddenly realized what was different. My room was filled with an orange glow. Why would that bother me? I started to think back through my life and try to recall if I had ever encountered an orange glow like this.

Yes, of course! The war! Every time the sun rose and set in the Saudi Arabian desert it would cast an orange glow over the entire desert. I also recalled that during the ground war we were patrolling through the desert in Kuwait at night and one of our own jets dropped a bomb on us. When it exploded the whole sky lit up in bright orange and it was just like daytime. These things were my orange glow.

I then realized that every time I encountered an orange glow now, my brain took me back to Saudi Arabia and the war. Hence, my heightened state of alert. I then had an understanding of why this was happening to me every time I saw orange. I was then able to deal with it every time it happened by telling myself I knew why it was occurring and it was ok because I was no longer in the war even though my brain kept taking me there.

However, things took an interesting turn. Every time I went into my bedroom thereafter I kept getting the panic attacks again even if there was no orange glow!

I then began to do some research on PTS. I found out that when one has a panic attack from a traumatic life event your brain re-records things and then "that" becomes the new memory. In other words, since this orange glow event happened in my bedroom, my bedroom was now part of my "war" memory.

Now, I had to change that memory. I had to make my bedroom "nice" again. Every time after that when I went into my bedroom I conducted relaxing activities, such as reading, writing, listening to jazz music. Thereby recreating my "nice" place and "re-recording" a good memory associated with my bedroom.

That is how I took my life back. One step at a time and one problem at a time. Remember, you have spent a good deal of time suffering from your trauma and re-recording things, which only added more and more to your primary issue. It added layer upon layer. This is what occurs when you ignore and/or self-medicate a problem. This occurs even if you are taking medication prescribed by a doctor because you are only numbing the emotion. You are not properly dealing with it and releasing it. You are only hiding from it. I should know, I spent 20 years numbing myself with alcohol and another 6 years numbing myself with psychotropic drugs prescribed by doctors. I never got any better until I quit doing those things and I learned my lesson from the orange glow and applied it.

For the second example I will describe my severe panic attacks I used to get in the grocery store. I have enjoyed cooking my whole adult life. Ever since I got out of the Marines, I would go to the grocery store as often as I could and buy good, fresh food in order to prepare myself a nice meal. It is something I really enjoy. However, for a period in my life it caused me great acrimony.

During the time I had PTS I would panic every time I got in a line at the checkout counter of the grocery store. I would freak out and run out of the store leaving my cart full of groceries. So, I started buying less food at a time and only going in the express lane when no one was in it, so I never had to stay in line. Then, the panic started happening when I was in the grocery store. Then it would happen in the parking lot and eventually it would happen at home once I would realize I needed to go grocery shopping. Every time this happened my brain re-recorded everything and it kept getting worse until I dealt with it.

I analyzed the situation. I discovered the reason I was panicking was because being in line made me feel claustrophobic. It reminded me of the fighting hole I lived in for a year during the war. Once it happened in line at the grocery store, my brain recorded where I was and it just got worse from there.

In order to cure myself, I decided to break this down into baby steps. First task was to get in my truck and drive to the grocery store. Then, the next day I actually parked my vehicle there. The third day I parked, got out of my vehicle and walked up to the front door. Each time I successfully completed my task, I congratulated myself for being strong and overcoming this. I repeated this process until I made it all the way through the whole experience without having a panic attack. Still, to this day, I use cooking a nice meal from scratch as an escape for myself. It's therapy for me. I took something back that gave me joy, which PTS had stolen from me. This greatly enhanced my confidence.

For my last example, I will discuss the little problem I developed with being in the dark. One of the classes I had in college was an astronomy class. It was fascinating and I really enjoyed it. One day the professor told us he had a treat for us and he was going to show us a movie. He then proceeded to turn the lights off. As soon as he did that, I completely panicked and ran out of the classroom.

It got worse as time went on. I started panicking every time I had that class. That morphed into panicking every time I was at school and so on. I knew what I had to do. I analyzed the situation. I understood that I was having problems because of the war.

I asked myself, "Why would the dark scare me at 26 years of age?" I then remembered that during the ground war the Iraqi's lit the oil fields of Kuwait on fire when we arrived there. It instantly got pitch black at 7am. It was so dark that I couldn't even see my hand in front of my face. We were all in the back of a dump truck. The Iraqi's then gassed us with nerve agent and since no one could see, people thought they inhaled the gas and began to panic.

Obviously, when the professor turned the lights off so quick it took my brain right back to that battle. I decided how I would deal with this. The very next semester I took a history of film course. We watched movies almost every class period, which was at night. I forced myself to face it because I understood what was happening and why. I really focused on the movies and their history. After the initial shock of it all, I really enjoyed that class. In fact, it became one of my favorites. Again, I took something back that PTS had stolen from me and turned it into something positive in my life that I enjoyed.

I was able to identify, deal with and overcome each one of these issues because I made myself "aware" of what was going on. I quit avoiding those things and faced them. Avoidance is one of the symptoms of PTS. I had taken the first few steps towards completely defeating PTS. I had laid the foundation to my healing journey which I took many years later without even realizing it. You can clearly see that "awareness" is a very important and necessary step.

I think this quote which I found in Carl Jung's book, "Memories, Dreams, Reflections," by Coleridge sums it all up pretty well. "He looked at his own Soul with a Telescope. What seemed all irregular, he saw and showed to be beautiful Constellations; and he added to the Consciousness hidden worlds within worlds."

Now, another part of awareness is to also pay attention to people you meet and the experiences that you have from those encounters. Nothing in life is circumstance. It all has a purpose and so do personal encounters. As I was writing this book I was also marketing my first two books. I had been spending many hours every day contacting newspapers, TV stations, radio stations, organizations, etc. It was one of those things that took a lot of effort for only a little reward. The more I did towards that effort the more it took me away from writing. I also developed a Facebook page and a twitter page. I reconnected with some old friends from childhood.

One day, several months later, one of those friends suggested that I set up a page on LinkedIn. So, I did. Then I developed a question to ask all the people I connected with. I simply asked if they had any suggestions on how to market my books. I sent out quite a few requests and I got one back from a fellow Veteran whom took the time to write a whole page to me about how to use social media to get myself out there instead of the old traditional email way I was doing it. I then realized the purpose of the connections I made with my old friend and this new Veteran friend. I abandoned my old Marketing plan and began to focus on the new one. My following really began to build. In fact, I still do it today.

However, there was more for me to learn, or to be "aware of". At the time, I was doing my own radio show. I had to drive two hours south every Saturday to do a one hour show. It took a lot of my time each week to do research and prepare the show. Now I had even more to do that was taking me away from my writing. The show cost me several hundreds of dollars a month to do. As fate would have it, I was driving home from the radio show one day on the freeway. Someone cut me off and caused me to get into a bad car accident. I was ok but I was very sore and cut up from the glass. My truck was totaled as well. This would cost more money as I would need to buy another vehicle.

The next couple days I was on the couch trying to heal. I was also dealing with some effects of my PTS because all the blood on my arm from the accident had awoken some dormant trauma from the war. I began to sit there and think while I was soar, tired, nauseous, nervous and having a hard time eating. There has to be some purpose for this. What could it be? I then realized that with all of these things I was doing the past year nothing was working out and bad things would happen. But why? Then it hit me. Because I was going in the wrong direction! These were all road blocks designed to "wake me up." Why you might ask? Because these were all things that were taking me away from what I was supposed to be doing, which was writing. As I mentioned in my previous book *Chrysalis*, when I was going through my healing process I had discovered my purpose in life, which was to write. My whole life had set me up for this task and now with all these other things I was doing, I was being pulled away from that task.

I began to refocus. I knew I would have to give up doing the radio show. I knew that I was supposed to stay involved in the stock market because that's how I make my money so that I can write. I know that I am supposed to spend the rest of my time after the market closes writing, doing research and learning, which all aid my mission in life to write. I still work some on building my following through social media like my new Veteran friend taught me. It takes about an hour to do so it frees me up to focus on what I need to. However, I did think to myself why did I get the opportunity to do this radio show? Not just simply to point me back in the right direction? There had to be another reason as well. There was. The 23rd Veteran concept was developed. That's what came out of that and when I was talking to the station manager on the phone about the radio show ending, this all hit me. Because of all of this, I was driven towards developing the title of my book and acquiring the bulk of material I would need to write this book. I can look back at all of these things I have done, how they didn't work out and how each time there were two purposes for it. The first was to let me know I was getting off track and the second was that I was also supposed to learn and take something from the experience. Paying attention to the events of your life, who you meet and the results, are also a very important part of your awareness.

These lessons I have just explained to you are also exacerbated in a poem written by Paulo Coelho in his book, "Warrior of the Light." It goes as follows:

> A warrior of the light knows that certain moments repeat themselves. He often finds himself faced by the same problems and situations, and seeing these difficult situations return, he grows depressed, thinking that he is incapable of making any progress in life. "I have been through all of this before," he says to his heart. "Yes, you have been through all this before," replies his heart. "But you have never been beyond it." Then the warrior realizes that these repeated experiences have but one aim: to teach him what he does not want to learn.

Therefore, you must become a student of your own life, learn from it and master it.

Awareness is knowing with conviction that everything that has happened to you is for the divine purpose of preparing you for your next step in life. It is having the ability to perceive that the energy of life exists in eternal perpetuity and it does not succumb to the same fate that all material and physical things do. So it is with this knowledge that you arm yourself as you begin each day knowing that you are one step closer to achieving your desires and that you will be guided along the way if you are willing to pay attention to the evidence which exists in your life.

AWARENESS
A
Worldly
Alertness
Releasing
Explanations

Numbing
Every
Social
Stigma

AWARENESS

3). POSITVE THINKING

    The very next step is to make a shift towards positive thinking, learn from your experiences and subsequently apply that to your life. By switching to positive thinking, I mean that you must learn to understand that every life experience you have had, good and bad, is a learning opportunity. Once you have this understanding you will then be able to turn every experience you have into something positive.

    I can personally tell you the reason why I have met every single person in my life. For example, marrying my ex-wife when I was in the Marines ended up bringing me back to Arizona after I got out of the military and moved back to Michigan. I had found out she was pregnant and subsequently, after I moved back to Arizona, I found out the baby wasn't mine. To most people this would be considered a horrible experience. It was for me at first. However, now that I understand I must reflect on my life and learn from it, I know there was a reason for it.

    Like I said, that experience brought me back to Arizona. After being back for a while, I started a landscape maintenance company. After doing that for a few years, I wanted to expand the business. That led me to enroll in a landscape architecture program in college. Once there, I immediately became interested in archaeology. I then switched my degree program accordingly. This got me a job working for the City at a local museum cleaning toilets and taking admission fees. Once there, I met the City Archaeologist and I transferred to Arizona State University. While I was finishing my degree I got to know the City Archaeologist quite well and even did a little work for him.

When I finally got my degree in Anthropology with an emphasis on archaeology from Arizona State, I got promoted to Assistant City Archaeologist. Once that occurred, the City Archaeologist began to hone my analytical skills and teach me how to write. After nearly 10 years of all this training, learning and experience, I felt like I was going nowhere because I knew I could never become the City Archaeologist because I did not have a graduate degree in Anthropology. This is required to obtain an archaeological permit, which was a requirement to get that job. I wanted to quit so bad, but something kept telling me that I had to stay, that there was more that I needed to learn and that when the time was right I would know for sure when to leave.

It's a good thing I listened to that feeling. Simply because at that point 9/11 had occurred and my boss convinced me, over a period of several months, to write a book about my experiences on the front lines of the first Gulf War *(A line in the Sand* www.robertserocki.com). It took me six years to write that book. After that, I eventually lost my job, my two houses, filed bankruptcy and then the slate was clean to start a whole new life. This led to the publication of my second book (***Chrysalis*** www.robertserocki.com) where I chronicled my struggles with, and overcoming, PTS. That all led me to the publication of this book, TV appearances, radio appearances, my own radio show, new partnerships, becoming a Veterans advocate and a whole new life where I am happier than I ever have been and truly at peace.

You can clearly see that shifting towards positive thinking, understanding that every experience you have had, has a reason and a lesson. Then reflecting upon that can provide wonderful consequences for you that can propel you into a rewarding, successful, happy life if you just have the right positive attitude and pay attention.

Another plethora of information I tapped into was my dreams. The same boss I had at the museum also turned me onto Carl Jung. He was an expert on dream analysis. So, I bought just about every book Jung ever wrote and began to study his methods (his books are listed in the PTS resources page in the back of this book). While I was doing this, I kept a journal of every dream I had for several years. I kept it on the night stand by me bed. Every time I woke up from a dream, I would write it down. Quite often, when we dream we are working out conflicts we are having in our lives that we may never even be aware of unless we analyze our dreams. They are a treasure trove of useful information. This whole process is outlined in great detail, including my dreams, in my book ***Chrysalis*** (www.robertserocki.com).

Now having said all of this and outlining this process you must begin to apply the things you have learned to your life and start acting upon them. By now, I am sure you can understand that I was having all of these experiences and learning things from them. I enhanced my focus and I applied what I was learning to each and every stage of my life. As I did that, it would lead to something bigger and better. Of course, it has been a bumpy ride riddled with strife. But I even took those experiences, analyzed them, asked myself what I could learn from them and then applied that knowledge as well. Thereby, eventually turning ***all*** of my experiences into positive ones. This is something I still religiously practice in my life today.

Positive thinking comes with your awareness of self. It is having conviction that there is a lesson embedded in every event, encounter, and experience in your life. Part of your human experience is having the cognitive ability to look back and reflect upon these occurrences with the notion that there is something you can learn from it and apply it to the next step in your life. Therefore, perceiving all the events of your life as petri dishes to facilitate the growth of bacterium that is analogous to growth and learning. Thereby, accepting each instance as a generous and gracious gift that promotes your physical and spiritual growth which is a necessary component of your physical existence here on Earth.

POSITIVE
Preparing
Our
Sentient
Intellect
To
Intuitively
View
Everything

POSITIVE

4). GRATITUDE

Now, after shifting to a positive way of thinking you must begin to have gratitude for what you do have. Be grateful and thankful for having a place to live and for food no matter how small or little those things are. Be grateful that you were able to acquire this book and that you have the strength to read it and take the first step in completing your journey. Be grateful for all the experiences you have had and all the things you have learned, etc.

All of your experiences, dreams, people you have met and material things you have, or have had, are truly blessings and gifts. Things given to you to help you along your way to achieving your purpose/passion in life. These things must be perceived as such. You must practice being grateful/thankful. I take time almost every night when I go to bed to actually say thank you for everything in my life. I am especially thankful for my ability to perceive things as I do and for being able to learn how to do this. Remember, no matter how bad you think you have it, someone always has it worse. Especially the person who has not taken the time to be a student of their life and to be grateful for it. Obviously, being grateful is homologous with being humble and being humble is a very good character trait indeed. It definitely lends itself to being happy with yourself and your life. You will then become most grateful, as I did, to perceive life in such a way.

When evidence of your desires manifests itself into your physical life you must graciously relinquish sincere thankfulness and appreciation for those gifts which you are about to receive. Accept them with humility for the awe inspiring force which brought them to you knowing that this giving and reciprocation is never ending. Never take anything for granted and nothing occurs by mere coincidence. Know this, be forever grateful and the cornucopia of living a divinely inspired life will always be open to you.

GRATITUDE
Graciously
Relinquishing
Accolades
To
Inspirational
Thought
Underlying
Divine
Efficacy

GRATITUDE

5). RETRAIN YOUR BRAIN
The very next step you need to undertake with this new "awareness" of yourself that you have, is to retrain your brain. Your brain was trained to have the reactions/responses it had during your trauma because they saved your life. Your brain was learning (i.e., being trained) how to react to these stimuli in such a way that would increase your survival. Your brain records the actual event, noises, smells, colors, animals, plants, people, etc. That way, when you encounter any one of these things again in the future your "learned" responses to these stimuli move into action. Just like the experiment Pavlov did with his dogs and the bells that we discussed in an earlier chapter.

Furthermore, as you go through your life after your trauma, your brain still has this recorded data base so to speak. Therefore, any time you encounter one of these stimuli the rest of your life your "learned" responses are enacted and your brain then re-records the trauma in a whole new environment. It records everything around you wherever you are at when these responses are triggered. This then becomes your new, updated, learned trauma. So, you can see how if this is not properly dealt with, the problem grows in magnitude, severity and in layers. Think of it like an onion. It is in layers. The longer you let this "grow," the more layers you will have to peel back in order to get to the "core" of the problem. I know, I spent more than 20 years adding to my trauma. This is precisely why you must begin to start retraining your brain in the early stages of your journey because it's going to take time to peel back all of those layers. It took time to get this way and it will take time to heal. Remember, your brain was "trained" to react this way. Therefore, it can be "retrained" in the same manner. Only this time you are taking a more active role in your development. What this simply means is that you are now beginning to take control of your life instead of succumbing to the effects of your PTS. Essentially, you are making the statement to yourself that enough is enough and that you are going to take back that which was taken from you in the first place.

A good example of this is the story I previously told about how I had problems with the color orange. Once I had an awareness of myself, what was going on and why, I was able to begin addressing the problem by recreating relaxing events in my bedroom. Thereby taking my bedroom back and making it a peaceful place once again as well as overcoming my panic response to the stimuli orange.

Another example is the story I told you about how I used to panic in the grocery store checkout line, which eventually led to me being afraid to even leave my house. Again, once I achieved an awareness of what was going on, I was able to address the problem. I had to do it in steps/layers, a little bit at a time as to not completely overwhelm myself. I started by getting into my truck, driving to the grocery store and parking. That was all I did the first day. My confidence in myself and my control over my reactions began to grow. Each time I went to the store thereafter, I increased what I did a little bit until I finally made it through the whole experience of grocery shopping and going through the checkout line without panicking and running out of the store. Now, I go all kinds of places and enjoy myself without incident. This is called, "retraining your brain."

To retrain yourself and your brain is to take back that which your trauma has taken from you. Your brain has learned through association and then creates an advanced perception to react in certain ways in order to protect you from future harm. Therefore, you can retrain it to see the world as a peaceful place once again. The human body has an inherent ability to heal itself as long as it gets the proper nutrition and thus proportionately so does your brain as long as you provide it with what it needs. Know this to be true, as evidence of this birth, death and re-growth is everywhere. You see it in nature, animals, outer space, planets, stars, and the human body.

Your answers and thus what you need are everywhere if only you can learn to see them. Everything is perfectly provided for you if you retrain your brain to properly focus on that which is evident. You must retrain your brain to develop new habits and to abandon the old. Shed the things that numb your existence, poison you, and those that provide you with a false sense of reality. Those things themselves are false and only take you further from your source and they provide a barrier to keep you disconnected which then begins to cause an internal physical decay of the divine vehicle you have been graciously provided with. This old behavior sends the message that you have completely forgotten about that from which you came. So, discard it and retrain yourself in this new enlightened manner.

RETRAIN
Reversing
Everything
The
Reactions
And
Internal
Nightmares

RETRAIN

6). GET HEALTHY
    Now it's time to work on getting your body healthy for optimum performance in whatever you do and to just feel good, which is something you probably haven't felt in a while if you are suffering from PTS. There are two basic ways to optimize your health. One is to eat a healthy, well balanced diet. The Second, is exercise!
    As a general rule, as far as eating healthy goes, try to consume foods that are organic, grass fed and that do not contain antibiotics, GMO's, hormones, etc. These things will just counteract everything you are trying to do, not to mention make you feel crummy. Now, you're probably not going to be able to make sure that every single thing you buy is organic. However, if most of what you eat is, you will be much better off and just fine. Like I keep saying, everything in moderation. It also depends on the stores that you have available to you in the area in which you live. Also, you can grow much of your own produce and herbs at home if you have the time and the place to do it. I try my best to make sure my food is organic and chemical free, but not everything is. I am ok with that and I still feel great. I also try to make sure that I do not consume any processed foods accept on occasion. So, if I go to a ball game I get a hotdog. It's ok. It's not going to hurt me because I only eat things like that once in a while. You don't have to be completely anal about this, but the more you stick to these

guidelines the better you will feel and conversely when you do eat garbage you will feel it.

Finally, on the subject of diet. Vitamin and mineral supplements are only to be taken as a way to top yourself off and not as your only nutritional intake. Also be sure to drink plenty of water. I like purified water as all of the chemicals are removed. If I drink tap water, I get serious heart burn. There is a reason for that. My body is telling me that the tap water is garbage because of the chemicals. For instance, they put fluoride in water. However, it's not the natural fluoride from the earth, it's a chemical version of it which is no good for you if you swallow it! They say that each day you should drink 64oz of water and if you exercise you may need up to 96oz of water.

As far as exercise goes, I mean both physical and mental. Just choose any sort of exercise that you like to do that works for you. It can be walking, running, hiking, rowing, etc. It doesn't matter. I myself like to run and hike. The important thing is that you do something. You should try to get at least 30 minutes of exercise a day. The more the better, but you must work up to higher levels at a moderate pace. Too much too soon will only cause you to give up as the task will seem to onerous. Increase your level and time as you feel comfortable. Remember, this is not a race. It's just about doing something every day towards a healthy you. As long as you are doing that, you are doing better than most people.

Good mental exercises are meditation and yoga like we previously discussed. Also, conducting your passion is a great way to partake in mental exercise. We will talk more about that in step number eight. I also meditate every night at bedtime and I perform a few basic yoga steps each morning. My passion is my writing, cooking, and the stock market. I do these things almost every day and they give me great joy and satisfaction as well as an internal peace.

HEALTH
Happily
Existing
Accepting
Living
Through
Harmony

HEALTH

Your body is a temple ever so perfectly created for you by your divine source. Therefore, why would you constantly poison it? When you take care of your body with proper nutrition and physical activity you give yourself the opportunity to connect with your source and to live in perfect harmony with all that is around you. This then puts you back in place so that you may receive that which you need in order to complete the tasks that you have been put here to complete. By being healthy you put yourself back in place in the cycle of life that guides all things. You no longer live as a single being experiencing that which occurs around you. You realize this and become a necessary part of all of it just as all pieces of a puzzle fit perfectly together. Thus, so do you in the cycle of life.

MEDITATION
Mind
Exposed
Divine
Inspiration
Total
Assimilation
Transcendent
Information
Occurring
Naturally

MEDITATION

Meditation is a stillness of the mind which allows for the transcendence of your spirit from an elemental plane of existence to a divine one. It is the connection of a conduit which opens up a pathway where information and energy for your soul flows from your eternal source. This connection must be maintained regularly to allow for the growth of your internal energy. This manifestation of source is a connection to the deific wisdom that resides in all matter. Because of this, your spiritual edification is limitless in both time and space. Therefore, your life has no boundaries except those which are humanly created. This allows you to understand that the human body is only a physical vehicle which houses that which has the ability to transcend time and space. It allows the internal self to escape all pain and suffering in order to occupy a space of peace and tranquility which has no boundaries and is limitless.

7). PEACE

Your very next step is to find/create peace for yourself. This is something you can do anywhere, anytime. For example, when I get really stressed I like to hike in the desert mountains by my house. I hike out to a spot where I am mostly alone and I sit and observe nature. I watch the animals, look at the plants and view the mountains. Next thing you know, I have forgotten about what was bothering me and I am revived by nature itself. It is very peaceful.

Nature is a place which reveals that the energy of life is eternal. It can answer all of life's questions. It is a tonic that heals your soul. It's a place which invokes thought and precipitates a deep spiritual connection. Nature is the circle of life. It is where all things begin and end only to begin again, hence bringing life itself to full circle.

NATURE
Nurturing
All
Throughout
U
Relinquishing
Everything

NATURE

I also will meditate during the day. I do this by playing nice music and closing my eyes and breathing deeply. I concentrate on the music and it takes me away just like nature does. Or, I sit outside and stare at a flower or some other plant, I concentrate on it and breathe deeply. The same thing happens. Also, doing what I love to do every day brings me great peace and joy that can't be recreated anywhere. So, if you are following me, I spend just about my entire day at peace without even realizing it by doing these things every day. You can achieve this too. It's all about making different choices and then enacting them. Most choices involve risk at some level or another. No risk, no reward. The greater the risk, the greater the reward. I can hear people now saying, "I don't like to take risks." My answer to that is, you already took some big risks to get yourself into the position you are in now. So why wouldn't take another big risk that will have good results instead of the bad ones you are experiencing now? Remember, once you hit your bottom, there is only one direction you can go and that is up!

Peace is existing in a perpetual state of calmness having the understanding that life is much more than a human existence. It provides great solace in knowing that what you need will be provided for you when you need it. Therefore, releasing you from all troublesome worry. It is knowing that there is something much more magnanimous that exists than you and I. Peace is the ability to transcend the mundane and live in harmony with something that most sentients cannot perceive to exist.

PEACE
Peacefully
Existing
As
Calm
Envelopes

PEACE

8). FIND YOUR PASSION
By now you are probably pretty sick of hearing me say "find your passion." The reason I say that is because this is probably one of the most important things you can do not only to heal your PTS, but to have a wonderful, great, rewarding, successful life. It's a real simple concept. Just do what makes you happy. Like Nike says, "Just do it!" As I already mentioned to you, for me it's writing, cooking and the stock market. When I do these things I am happy and completely focused. When I am doing these things I forget about my problems. The world five inches from my face and beyond is non-existent for me. In other words your passion will do several things for you, such as bring you joy, help you to escape, find peace, release your emotions and to accomplish all of the things that your heart desires.

Your passion can be anything you choose. You can write, paint, draw, play guitar, sing, sky dive, hike, raise gold fish, train dogs, etc. Don't worry if it sounds silly or too complicated. If it's what makes you happy, if it's what makes you want to get out of bed in the morning, then the bad things people tell you and negative things they do won't matter. You will be happy and that's what counts. It's like a friend's father once told me when I was talking to him about a career choice I was making. I was going to school to be an archaeologist. Everyone told me not to do it because I would never get a job. At least not one that paid me to do it. My friend's father told me that if it put a fire in my belly, I should do it. Most people do not love what they do and if you do, you will be successful at it for that reason. So, I took his advice and I got my degree in Anthropology with an emphasis in archaeology. True to his word, two weeks after I started college I got a paid job working at a museum cleaning toilets and taking admission fees. It wasn't archaeology per say, but it got my foot in the door. Over the course of the next 16 years I worked my way up to Assistant City Archaeologist and I was making great money and had full benefits. Now, if I would have listened to the nay sayers, I would have missed out on that. I would have also missed out on one very important thing. By doing archaeology, I learned how to write and conduct research, which eventually led me to my life's passion of writing books and a rewarding new career.

So, the moral of the story is, FIND YOUR PASSION and do it. The hell with what anyone else says. It's your life and YOU are the one that has to live it and pay the price for living it. So, no one else's opinion on that matters. They don't have to live your life. Also remember that misery loves company. So most of the time the people that shoot down your dreams and goals are miserable themselves and they want you to be that way too. Last time I checked, this was still America and you can do anything or be whatever you want here within the boundaries of the law, as long as you are willing to work for it.

Your passion is the thing that puts a fire in your belly. It's the thing or things you are called to do every day. This is something you feel you must do each and every day and when you don't your life just doesn't seem right. It's the magnet that constantly draws you to it with a power that seems irresistible. Your passion is what you were put on earth to do to enhance humanity. It is the song that resides within you. Let it out and allow it to blossom like a flower. The biggest mistake you can make is to expire with your song still left inside you.

PASSION
Positive
Activities
Serving
Spirit
Inspiration
Orchestrated
Naturally

PASSION

9). PROCESS YOUR EMOTIONS

An important aspect of processing your emotions is dream analysis. I kept a journal by my bed for many, many years. Every time I awoke from a dream I wrote it down in my book no matter what time it was. Then, I would go back later and try to analyze the dream and figure out what it was trying to teach me. In fact, I still do this. I get many inspirational ideas from my dreams and important lessons about my life. It is a tool that you are given for free. Therefore, you must learn to use it wisely and it can be a powerful and very effective tool in your tool box. As with all things in life, it takes time to learn to use this "tool" properly. I read many books about the subject and practiced constantly what I learned. It has served me well. As I previously mentioned my favorite expert on the subject is Carl Jung. In fact much of my second book, Chrysalis, is about my dream analysis which I learned from studying his books. I will share a quote with you from ***Chrysalis***. It is one I borrowed from CG Jung's book, ***Dreams***.

Dreams of modern man bring him memories, insights, experiences, awaken dormant qualities in our personality, and reveal the unconscious element in our relationships. So, it seldom happens that anyone who has taken the trouble to work over his dreams with qualified assistance for a longer period of time remains without enrichment and a broadening of his mental horizon.

I have acquired a great deal of enrichment and broadening of my mental horizon in my life thru analysis of my dreams. I continue to do so even to this day. It is a powerful tool at your disposal. For instance, I learned from my dreams that the war I was involved in would eventually kill me from the inside if I did not deal with it properly. I also learned that I needed to quit drinking so much alcohol as it was only numbing my problems, causing additional problems and was not curing the main issue I was dealing with, which was the PTS. I also learned that I needed to be a healthier individual. I needed to eat better, exercise and get plenty of vitamins and nutrients. I also learned that I needed to learn to relax and calm myself through meditation, music and releasing my emotionally charged memories.

Furthermore, I figured out what I was supposed to do with my life. I figured out my purpose in life. Everything I went through then began to make sense to me. I also received insights to future events in my life. Some of which have already happened and others I am still waiting for them to come to fruition. I simply cannot fathom living the rest of my life without utilizing this very important tool we all have been graciously given. As human beings we have so many things at our disposal, yet we ignore most of them as nonsensical absurdity. Why? Societal stigmas I guess. All this does is limit you from achieving your full potential. So why let it? I can't help but think this is relative to what scientists say about our brains. They say that we only actually use something like 10% of our brain. The rest of it is untapped potential! To me life is the same. We only probably use a very small percentage of the "tools" that are available to us. The rest just sits idle, wasting away.

Now, if you are like me when I was dealing with my trauma, you are having bad nightmares. Your brain understands that you are having problems, that something is wrong. Your brain is doing two things. It is trying to work out the problem while you are sleeping when nothing else is bothering you and it is trying to get your attention and let you know that you need to deal with these things. This is why writing your dreams down is so important.

That way you can go back to it later and start dealing with your issues without having to worry about trying to remember your dream from eight hours ago, two days ago, etc.

Also, by writing these dreams down you have begun your healing process without you even knowing it. Because when you write these dreams down you are releasing your emotions! This is one of the next and most beneficial things you can learn to do for yourself. You must learn to release your emotions in healthy ways. You can achieve this through activities, such as playing an instrument, writing/singing a song, painting, drawing or writing books, poems, letters, etc. I do several of these things to help myself. However, for me, the most effective thing was writing.

It all started for me when my boss at work and my friends kept telling me I should write a book about my experiences on the front lines of the first Gulf War as a Marine. I blew it off for a long time until one day I decided to do it. I figured at the very least it would get this "story" off of my chest that I needed to tell and that every time someone asked me about the war, I could just hand them a book and I wouldn't have to talk about it. So, I wrote a book called, ***A Line in the Sand***. Little did I know at the time that this was only the beginning to my journey and not the end of it liked I was hoping.

That one simple technique of writing turned into me publishing three books including this one, appearances on TV and radio, articles and reviews written about me in newspapers, websites and magazines and my own radio show, 23rd Veteran, in which I discussed Veteran's issues. Writing did that for me because as I was writing I was releasing emotionally charged memories and I was healing. Each time I did that I was able to grow and build upon it. Thus, propelling me into the future and my current life.

Shortly after my first book my life took a horrible downturn, or so I thought. My PTS got worse and I ended up in the hospital. However, now that I can look back at this, it was the beginning of my real work and it was something that needed to happen in order for me to begin to grow and heal. So, with an understanding that I needed to get better, I moved forward with this. I had good days and bad, accomplishments and setbacks, but in the long run I came out on top and ahead. Quite simply put, I am happy. You can be too.

On one of my office visits with one of my doctors many years ago she taught me something very important and vital to my success in healing and thus life. She gave me some homework. We had been talking about people in my life whom had hurt me and treated me badly. My doctor, being astute ascertained that this was one of the many things that was bothering me and that added to the cornucopia of problems I was carrying around with me. So, she told me she wanted me to deal with this and release it. She told me she wanted me to go home and make a list of everyone and everything that has hurt me and what happened. Then she instructed me to feel the emotion so I could understand what these people and events were really doing to me. Finally, she said that after that was finished she wanted me to find a way to release those emotions in a healthy way so that I could move on. She told me I can use whatever gives me inspiration to complete this task.

So, I set out on my task. The next day I made my list. I went through the things on my list and experienced the emotions. I was so distraught that I became physically sick. I vomited. My bones and muscles began to ache like I had been run over by a truck. I cried uncontrollably. I was exhausted. I then had a setback and got drunk. After the next day, after allowing myself to feel bad, after letting it all out and understanding that this was ok because I had been through hell, I began the final stage of this one task.

I got out a pad of paper and a pen. I wrote a letter to everyone in life whom had hurt me. I let it all out. I did not hold back anything. I said whatever I felt. I even invented some new cuss words. When I was done with each letter I signed them. I then said, "I release you from my life. I am done with you and I am moving forward and I wish you the very best." Then I signed them. I let myself experience those emotions for a while. Then, I took each letter and went over to my trash can. I crumbled each letter up in my hand

and squeezed them so hard I think I squeezed all of the pulp out of the paper! I then said out loud to each letter, "I release you." I threw each one into the trash can. I took the bag out of the can and threw it into the dumpster. I was done with that problem. That was the best, biggest most important thing I ever did towards my healing process. That particular event led me to write my second book, ***Chrysalis***. I describe these events and many others in that book in great detail.

Basically, once you find your passion and start doing it, you can use it to release the emotion in your traumatic memories in healthy, positive ways. You then render those emotionally charged memories into just memories that no longer control your life. Therefore, you are taking back your life. By doing this, you can end up with a whole new career and a whole new, rewarding life without even knowing it just like what happened to me. I took everything that ever happened to me, every experience I ever had and used it towards accomplishing something positive. That process, which kept building upon itself led me to where I am today. If I never would have taken that first step towards healing, If I would have listened to everyone whom said you can't do that, If I would have listened to everyone whom said you can't heal from PTS, I would've have missed out on the biggest opportunity of my life… being truly happy and at peace.

In order to heal one must process their emotionally charged memories. You do this by releasing your emotion in healthy, natural ways. Thereby, turning emotionally charged memories into just memories. It is the expulsion of the calamitous trauma in your life. You must let yourself feel the charge in order for it to pass through you. You need a vehicle to transport these emotions from the depths of your soul out into the universe for dispersion in order to effect an inner peace.

This vehicle you use cannot be toxic or put up boundaries in any way. It must be something that gives you positive direction and compels you to complete your process. It must be something that allows you to flourish and that expands your mind and soul in all directions. Once these emotions are processed and released, the weight of a thousand mountains will be lifted from your chest and you will be ready to spring forward through the door of life with nothing to hold you back as you find your prosperity.

PROCESS
Precipitate
Release
Of
Calamitous
Emotions
Supporting
Serenity

PROCESS

10). FOCUS
    This next step is very basic. You just need to focus on the task at hand. Focus on yourself, your life and what you want to do with it. Focus on the goals you want to accomplish in your life. Quite frankly, part of the healing process is being selfish. By that I mean yes, you must focus on yourself in order to heal. In fact, any successful person will tell you that strict focus is one of the most important things that helped them to achieve their dreams. Without it, you will be distracted and you will never get anything accomplished. So, you must come up with a plan to stick to. This brings us to step 11 in the Foundation To Healing.
    An acute focus on your passion and your life is necessary to achieve the pinnacle of success. All barriers must be broken down. All societal stigmas must be dismissed. One understands that enacting their passion is first and foremost in the participation of their daily routine. Those things that distract you from your true calling are unnecessary and must be set aside to allow the proliferation of what fuels the fire of your soul. Your attention must be placed on this with an acute clarity which surpasses that

of even the most intense ocular focus. This focus then acts in a propulsionary manner towards the attainment of success.

FOCUS
Fathom
Opportunity
Cognize
Understand
Success

FOCUS

11) GOALS
Now that you have focused on the things you want to accomplish in your life, it is time to write them down. A person without a plan and focus will be all over the place. Nothing will ever get accomplished. Yes indeed, all plans change. They are dynamic things. As my Sergeant used to say, "Semper Gumby. Always flexible!" So you can see that if you set out to accomplish something and you have no focus and no goals you will be doomed from the start. You will never even accomplish step one. It is like building a house. If you do not build the foundation (your goals and focus) first, the house will crumble. If you do build the foundation (your goals and focus) the house will be able to withstand most anything. Even if something does come along and destroys the house, and that will happen sometimes, you still have the foundation to rebuild again. Without that foundation, you won't even be able to rebuild the house, just as without a foundation you would not be able to rebuild your life. Many successful people have built things and lost them. However, because they had focus and goals (your foundation) they were able to re-build again. Look at Jesse Livermore. He became very wealthy and lost it all. In fact, that happened three times. Look at Donald Trump. At one point in his life he was in debt to his ears and on the verge of total disaster. Yet,

he was able to rebuild again and now look at him. So, you must build your foundation.

You must write your goals down. It's a form of commitment. Every year on New Year's Eve I sit down and make a list of goals for the next 12 months. I write them down as though I have already accomplished them. No dream is too big for me. I dream as big as I want. If that's my goal, then I write it down. Most people say not to dream so big because if you don't accomplish that goal you will only get depressed and give up. On the contrary! The only thing that way of thinking does, is to program your brain to sell yourself short. You are only limiting yourself to what others say you can or can't do. Remember, it's your life. You have to live it.

I know that my possibilities are endless and that my success ONLY comes from whether or not I work hard enough to accomplish my goals and/or want it bad enough. So, I write these goals down. I usually write down 10. But you don't have to have any specific amount. You can just write down one goal if that is all you want to accomplish. Plus, by writing these goals down, you commit them to memory and you will work on them whether you realize it or not.

Your goals are a list of things you want to achieve in relation to your passion. As these goals are accomplished you are liberated through your success. That is why success is different for everyone. It is a very individual achievement. Something that only you would understand and comprehend as, eternal happiness and the reciprocation of gratitude for the opportunity to exist and to pursue your goals. It does not matter how big or grandiose they are because you understand that anything may be accomplished. Do not listen to the nay sayers, the people with negative energy, for no one but you can truly understand that these goals of yours are your own personal road map. They are part of the divine guidance bestowed upon you in order to effect the attainment of the things your soul craves. The completion of these desires are the sole purpose for your earthly existence. With that understanding you approach life with the conviction of knowing that you will be successful if you stick to your goals because nothing can possibly stand in your way.

GOALS
Guidance
On
Achievement
Liberating
Success

GOALS

12). REVIEW
Your list of goals needs to be reviewed. You can review your list of goals from time to time throughout the course of the next 12 months to gauge your progress if you wish. I however, write them down on New Year's Eve and I don't review them again until the following New Year's Eve. This is what works best for me. I don't always accomplish my goals to the level I had written down. That is ok. Because what actually happens when I review the list once a year is that I see just how far I actually came to accomplishing those huge goals in just 12 months. This makes me feel awesome that after one year I have actually come that far when most people can't even do that in a lifetime! This then motivates me to try even harder and to build upon those original goals. I don't get depressed and quit at all. In fact, I look forward to New Year's every year just so I can see how great I did trying to accomplish such huge goals that everyone said could never be done. For most people, New Year's is just an excuse to get drunk. Not for me!

From time to time, as often as is necessary, review your goals. When you do this, you will see just how far you have come towards their attainment, if you haven't attained them already. This review will energize your soul and help keep you on track towards accomplishing the things that are most important to you. It acts like a carrot being dangled in front of your nose that you want to catch in order to nourish your hungry soul. You understand that you will starve until you acquire this object. Therefore, you never let it out of your sight. You awake each day with the passion to pursue it until the ultimate glory besieges you and then the process begins again. It builds in layer upon layer. Thus, creating the foundation that will always ensure your success and well-being.

REVIEW
Refresh
Exult
Valuate
Internalize
Every
Wish

REVIEW

13). STAY CONNECTED
Lastly, as a human being you must stay connected. That's part of being human. Claude Levi-Strauss discusses this interconnectedness we have in his book, *"The Origin of Table Manners."* Remember, one of the symptoms of having PTS is isolation. You isolate yourself from family, friends, your community and the world. You justify this by telling yourself no one can ever understand what you have been through. Maybe they can't. So what. The hell with them and what they think. What matters is that YOU understand your problems and what you have been through. YOU are the only one that can fix them. This ties back into the very first step of this healing process, Acceptance.

So, you must fight this isolationist ideal by staying connected. You can accomplish this by watching the local news so you stay connected with your community and what's going on. You can watch the national news so you stay connected with what's going on in the world. You can read the paper. Yes, you may do these things while sitting alone in your home, but you are not letting the world pass you by.

Next, go for a walk. Say hi to people you pass on the street. Go volunteer on something that is important to you and your community. When you go to the store, or the post office say hi to the people who work there. Ask them how they are doing. Just make small talk. You don't have to get into any great debate. What you are doing is breaking down your isolationist barriers brick by brick. One step will lead to another and then next thing you know, you will be a social butterfly!

You also need to stay connected to your spirit and your inspiration. You stay connected to your spirit, or the energy within you by meditation, prayer, etc. Practice this every day. It's a way of recharging yourself by staying plugged in so to speak. You stay connected to your inspiration by following it. Do something towards achieving your goals (i.e., inspiration) every day.

Staying connected is the equivalent to staying plugged in. This is the conduit through which all of your divine inspiration and messages are sent to you. By not staying connected you facilitate the implementation of an internal decay. When you stay connected to spirit, you precipitate a growth and a knowing that transcends all boundaries and expels all worry. You begin to understand that you are part of a well prepared and highly organized plan. There is nothing to fear. There is no occasion for worry. You realize the only thing that exists which merits your attention is your connection to spirit. It provides you with the road map to build your foundation and successfully manifest your divine inspiration. Thus, bringing you and your life full circle. Hence, I leave you with my 13 step foundation to healing.

<u>CONNECTED</u>
Constant
Outlook
Never
Negating

Each
Chance
To
Elicit
Divinity

CONNECTED

Lastly, I would like to share with you an inspirational poem I wrote in March of 2014. I wrote it for a creative writing group whom were trying to heal from PTS through writing. I hope this propels you toward taking that first step on your journey to heal and become successful once again. The poem is called ***My Box***.

In my box I hide, safe and sound inside.
Barrier put up, outside denied.
Holding you back, staying with what's familiar, keeps you down, seems quite peculiar.
Focused on the negative, the box stays closed. I am my own worst enemy, I suppose.
Second guessing the opportunity to be successful, I am the only one who knows.
Staying focused on the past holds you back, as my box only shows.
So, I come out of my box and I discard my shield. My brightest future, as a sword, I must wield!
Hmmmm, my box.

CLOSING WORDS

This foundation to healing is not meant to be a set in stone must follow exactly as written plan. All plans, as all things, are dynamic. You can adapt these to what suits you best. It's your life. It's your journey. So, by all means personalize it. The important thing is that you have a foundation to begin from so you are not lost right from the start.

As with anything in life, do your research on whatever you do. Do your homework. Understand what you are doing and what the outcomes may be. You wouldn't simply go to war without understanding your enemy. That would simply be foolish. Everything in this book is based on my own experiences over the course of 25 years, all of the personal research I have conducted and my own results from applying that information and experience to my life. It's your life. You have to live it and live with the results of the choices you make. Success, and thus proportionately failure, are the direct results of decisions that you have made. No one else's. It's just that simple. So take responsibility for your own life. I would like to also say that I wish you the very best on your journey to healing and a happy life. I sincerely mean that.

This is something you CAN do even though most people will say you can't. I did it, so I know it can be done and I know that you CAN do it too.

Good luck and God speed.
Robert Serocki, Jr.
23rd Veteran
www.robertserocki.com

13 STEP FOUNDATION TO HEALING

1. ACCEPTANCE
2. AWARENESS
3. POSITIVE THINKING
4. GRATITUDE
5. RETRAIN YOUR BRAIN
6. GET HEALTHY
7. PEACE
8. FIND YOUR PASSION
9. PROCESS YOUR EMOTIONS
10. FOCUS
11. GOALS
12. REVIEW
13. STAY CONNECTED

PTS RESOURCE GUIDE

BOOKS

Coelho, Paulo. *"Warrior of the Light, A Manual: Short Notes on Accepting Failure, Embracing Life, and Rising to your Destiny."* New York, NY. Harper Perennial. 2003.

Dyer, Wayne Dr. *"Inspiration Your Ultimate Calling."* Carlsbad, Ca. Hay House, Inc. 2006.

Foa, Edna B., Terence M. Keane, Matthew J. Friedman and Judith A. Cohen, eds. *"Effective Treatments for PTSD: Practice Guidelines from the International Society for Traumatic Stress Studies, Second Edition."* New York, NY. The Guilford Press. 2009.

Isaacson, Walter. *"Benjamin Franklin: An American Life."* New York, NY. Simon and Schuster Paperbacks. 2003.

Jung, C.G.
    "Dreams." Princeton, New Jersey. Princeton University Press. Ninth printing. 1990.

"Memories, Dreams, Reflections." Edited by Aniela Jaffé and translated from German by Richard and Clara Winston. New York. Vintage books a division of Random House, Inc. 1989.

"The Undiscovered Self." New York, NY. Signet, an imprint of New American Library, Division of Penguin Group (USA) Inc. 2006.

Lawlis, Frank Dr. *"The PTSD Breakthrough: The Revolutionary, Science Based Compass Reset Program."* 2010.

Livermore, Jesse. Added Material by Richard Smitten. *"How to Trade in Stocks: The classic formula for understanding timing, money management, and emotional control."* New York, NY. McGraw-Hill. 2001.

Levi-Strauss, Claude. *"The Origin of Table Manners: Mythologiques, Vol.3."* Translated from French by John and Doreen Weightman. Chicago. The University of Chicago Press. 1990.

McCullough, David. *"John Adams."* New York, NY. Simon and Schuster. 2001.

Schiraldi, Glenn R., Ph.D. *"The Post-Traumatic Stress Disorder Sourcebook, second edition: A guide to healing, recovery, and growth."* McGraw-Hill. 2009.

Serocki, Jr. Robert A.

"A Line in the Sand: The true story of a Marine's experiences on the front lines of the first Gulf War." One World Press. 2006.

"Chrysalis: A metamorphosis has begun!" One World Press. 2014.

"The Sword and the Anvil: A definitive guide for natural, healthy healing from Post-Traumatic Stress and Trauma." One World Press. 2016.

Trump, Donald and Bill Zanker. *"Think Big and Kick Ass: In Business and in Life."* New York, NY. Collins. 2007.

WEBSITES

http://www.mayoclilnic.org/diseases-conditions/post-traumatic-stress-disorder/basics/coping-support/con-20022540http://www.ptsd.va.gov
http://www.edc.org
http://www.nih.gov
http://www.historyofptsd.wordpress.com
http://www.wikipedia.org
http://on.pnj.com/1w3ZoK9
http://www.medicalnewstoday.com
http://www.sciencedaily.com
http://en.wikipedia.org/wiki/long-term_effects_of_cannabis
http://en.wikipedia.org/wili/Medical_cannabis
http://en.wikipedia.org/w/index.php?title=Cortisol&printable=yes
http://drugabuse.gov
http://www.helpguide.org/articles/ptsd-trauma/post-traumatic-stress-disorder.htm
http://www.cchr.org
http://www.cchrint.org/psychiatric-drugs/antidepressantsideeffects
http://www.cchr.org/documentaries/the-hidden-enemy/psychiatric-drugs-cause-suicide.html
http://www.cchr.org/documentaries/the-hidden-enemy/antipsychotics-sudden-deaths.html
http://www.cchr.org/documentaries/the-hidden-enemy/experimenting-on-troops.html
http://authoritynutrition.com/11-proven-benefits-of-olive-oil/
http://authoritynutrition.com/10-healthy-herbs-and-spices/
http://authoritynutrition.com/10-proven-benefits-of-spirulina/
http://draxe.com/naturally-reverse-cavities-heal-tooth-decay/

www.vitamindcouncil.org
www.nutritionexpress.com
www.livestrong.com
www.drweil.com
www.bestnaturalfoods.com
www.chriskresser.com/vitamin-k2-the-missing-nutrient/
http://msutoday.msu.edu/news/2014/yoga-helps-former-marine-msu-student-recover-from-ptsd/
http://casapalmera.com/6-natural-ways-to-treat-anxiety/

ARTICLES

American Academy of Sleep Medicine. "Cognitive behavioral therapy for insomnia reduces suicidal thoughts in veterans." Science Daily. Science Daily, 2 February 2015. http://www.scinecedaily.com/releases/2015/02/150202114632.htm

American Friends of Tel Aviv University. "Acute psychological stress reduces ability to withstand physical pain. "Science Daily. Science Daily, 5 February 2015. http://www.sciencedaily.com/releases/2015/02/150205111806.htm

American Pain Society. "Mediation can reduce chronic neck pain, study shows." ScienceDaily. ScienceDaily, 24 February 2015. www.sciencedaily.com/releases/2015/02/150225094105.htm.

American Psychological Association (APA). "Suicide prevention requires access to effective, evidence-based treatment. "Science Daily. Science Daily, 18 September 2014. http://www.science-daily.com/releases/2014/09/140918141159.htm

American Society of Anesthesiologists (ASA). "Common anesthetic procedure dramatically improves well-being of veterans with PTSD." Science Daily. Science Daily, 11 October 2014. http://www.sciencedaily.com/releases/2014/10/141011172042.htm

Basu, Moni. CNN. "Why suicide rate among veterans maybe more than 22 a day." November 14, 2013. http://www.cnn.com/2013/09/21/us/22veteran-suicides-a-day/

Casa Palmera. "6 Natural Ways to Treat Anxiety." November 6, 2014. http://casapalmera.com/6-natural-ways-to-treat-anxiety/

Cox, David. "Unbroken: What makes some people more resilient than others?" The Guardian, 19 December 2014. http://www.theguardian.com/uk

Davis, Kathleen. "How to control panic attack symptoms." Medical News Today. MediLexicon, Intl. 4 Mar. 2015. Web. 4 Mar. 2015. http://www.medicalnewstoday.com/articles/290177.php

Davis, Marketta and Rob Johnson. "The VA unwittingly scares PTSD victims." Pensacola News Journal. October 13, 2014. http://www.pnj.com

Ellis, Marie. "Misfiring in the brain's control system linked to OCD." Medical News Today. MediLexicon, Intl. 19 December 2014. Web. 19 Dec 2014. http://www.medicalnewstoday.com/articles/287291.php

Eth, Zurich. "How early trauma influences behavior." Science Daily. Science daily, 1 December 2014. http://www.sciencedailycom/releases/2014/12/141201125158.htm

Innes, Wendy. Independent Voter Network (IVN). "Over 80% of Veterans with PTSD believe current VA treatment is ineffective." December 4, 2014. http://www.ivn.us/2014/12/04/80

Kime, Patricia. Military Times. "Troops sleep problem may be new disorder." October 30, 2014. http://www.militarytimes.com/article/20141030/BENEFITS06/310300047

Kinder, Tabatha, IBTimes. "Israeli arms treats 700 soldiers with PTSD symptoms after fighting in Gaza." IBTimes, UK, November 5, 2014. http://www.ibtimes.co.uk/israeli-arms-treats-700-soldiers-ptsd-sumptoms-after-fighting-gaza-1473273

McGuire, Marsden, M.D., Deputy Chief Consultant, Mental Health Standards of Care; Paula Schnurr, Ph.D., Acting Executive Director, National Center for PTSD, Tracy L. Smith, Ph.D., Psychotherapy Coordinator Office of Patient Care Services, Veterans Health Administration, Department of Veterans Affairs. "Prolonged Exposure: A first-line treatment for PTSD. January 27, 2015. http://www.ptsd.va.gov

Medical University of Vienna. "Trigger for stress processes discovered in brain." Science Daily. Science Daily, 27 November 2014. http://www.sciencedaily.com/releases/2014/11/141127082309.htm

Mitchell, Heidi. "Mediterranean diet counters aging effects on the brain." Wall Street Journal. 12 May 2015.

Murphy, Jen. "Yoga and strength training brings creativity to the table." Wall Street Journal. 12 May 2015.

National Institute on Drug Abuse: The Science of drug abuse and addiction. "Drug facts: Marijuana." Revised January 2014. http://www.drugabuse.gov/publications/drugfacts/marijuana

Nichols, Hannah. "Protein sustains both a sound mind and a strong heart." Medical News Today. MediLexicon, Intl., 13 Jan. 2015. Web. 14 Jan. 2015. http://www.medicalnewstoday.com/articles/287910.php

Rand Corporation. "Mental health providers not well prepared to care for military veterans, study finds." Science Daily. Science

Daily, 12 November 2014. http://www.sciencedaily.com/releases/2014/11/141112102638.htm

Reddy, Sumathi. "A diet might cut the risk of developing Alzheimer's." Wall Street Journal. 21 April 2015.

Reno, Jamie. "Medicating our troops into oblivion: Prescription drugs said to be endangering U.S. soldiers. International Business Times. 19 April 2014.

Reickhoff, Paul. Huffington Post. "22 a day is unconscionable: Preventing veteran suicide." September 9, 2014. http://www.huffingtonpost.com/paul-reickhoff/22-a-day-is-unconscionable_b_5793528.html

Rosenbaum, Simon. The Conversation. "Working out PTSD-exercise is a vital part of treatment." December 12, 2014.

Rosenthal, Michele. "10 Tips for understanding someone with PTSD." Heal my PTSD blog. January 20, 2015.

Tartakovsky, M. (2015). The Power in Being Still & How to Practice Stillness. *Psych Central*. Retrieved on January 7, 2015, from http://psychcentral.com/blog/archives/2015/01/07/the-power-in-being-still-how-to-practice-stillness/

Tata Institute of Fundamental Research. "Neuronal encoding of the switch from specific to generalized fear." Science Daily. Science Daily, 1 December 2014. http://www.sciencedaily.com/releases/2014/12/141201113124.htm

UCSF Benioff Children's Hospital Oakland. "Omega-3 fatty acids, vitamin D may control brain serotonin, affecting behavior and psychiatric disorders." ScienceDaily. ScienceDaily, 25 February 2015. www.sciencedaily.com/releases/2015/02/150225094109.htm

University of Buffalo. "Positive personality traits may protect police at high risk for PTSD." Science Daily. Science Daily, 6 January 2015. http://ww.sciencedaily.com/releases/2015/01/150106104136.htm

University of Melbourne. "Diet, nutrition essential for mental health." ScienceDaily. ScienceDaily, 29 January 2015. www.sciencedaily.com/releases/2015/01/150129104217.htm

University of Pittsburgh Graduate School. "Personalized medicine to reduce adverse drug outcomes in people with mental Illness." Medical News Today. MediLexicon, Intl., 4 Feb 2015. Web. 4 Feb. 2015. http://medicalnewstoday.com/releases/288929.php

University of Texas Health Science Center. "Study finds short-term psychological therapy reduces suicide attempts in at-risk soldiers." Medical News Today. MediLexicon, Intl., 18 Feb. 2015.web.

Universität Mainz. "New theoretical framework for future studies of resilience." Science Daily. Science Daily, 27 January 2015. http://www.sciencedaily.com/releases/2015/01/150127100349.htm

Veterans Health Administration. "VA doctors looking for new ways to treat PTSD." http://www.va.gov./health/newsFeatures/20120712a

Wagner, Dennis. The Arizona Republic. "Arizona veteran suicides a tragic cost of broken VA system." August 24, 2014. http://www.azcentral.com/story/news/arizona/investigations/2014/08/24

Walser, Adam. ABC Action News. "Veteran says he was repeatedly put on hold by veterans' suicide hotline." April 13, 2015. http://www.abcactionnews.com

Whiteman, Honor. "Skunk linked to increased risk of psychosis." Medical News Today. MediLexicon, Intl., 17 Feb 2015. Web. 18 Feb 2015. http://www.medicalnewstoday.com/articles/289555.php

Yehuda, Rachel, Ph.D. "Post-Traumatic Stress Disorder." N Engl J Med, Vol. 346, No.2. January 10, 2002. http://www.nejm.org

Zoroya, Gregg, USA Today. "Rise in PTSD cases from two wars strains resources." November 29, 2011. http://www.usatoday.com/news/military/story/2011-11-29/PTSD-cases-rise/5147660

PRESS RELEASES

Miller, Jeff, Chairman House Committee on Veterans Affairs. "Statement on VA's Refusal to fire VA scandal figure Sharon Helman." Nov 4, 2014. http://veterans.house.gov/press-release/chairman-miller-statement-on-va-s-refusal-to-fire-va-scandal-figure-sharon-helman

Porter, Mokie. Vietnam Veterans of America. "VA turns back on C-123 crews poisoned by toxic herbicides." April 16, 2015. http://www.vva.org/PressReleases/2015/pr15-005.html

REPORTS

Office of Inspector General, Department of Veterans Affairs, Office of Health Care Inspections. "Suicide Risk and Alleged Medical Management Issues Hampton VA Medical Center Hampton, Virginia. Report No. 14-02139-156. March 30, 2015. http://www.va.gov/oig

www.ingramcontent.com/pod-product-compliance
Lightning Source LLC
Chambersburg PA
CBHW020034120526
44588CB00030B/280